Strike While the Iron is Hot

Strike While the Iron is Hot

Three plays on sexual politics
edited and introduced
by
Michelene Wandor

The Journeyman Press
London & West Nyack

First published by the Journeyman Press, 1980
97 Ferme Park Road, Crouch End, London N8 9SA and
17 Old Mill Road, West Nyack, NY 10994

British Library Cataloguing in Publication Data

Strike While the Iron is Hot.
   1. English drama - 20th century
   2. Women - Drama
   I. Wandor, Michelene
   822'.91'409352   PR1272

ISBN 0-904526-47-X

*Photoset by Dessett Graphics and
printed by Interlink Longraph, London*

INTRODUCTION

The plays in this book have all emerged from the socialist theatre movement in Britain during the last ten years. It is a cultural movement which challenges the conventional demarcation between artistic self-expression and a political commitment to changing society; and all three plays are evidence of the impact which feminist and gay activism have had on and within socialist theatre.

Theatre and performance have always been used by emerging political movements to express and support their struggles, both in street- and agitprop theatre forms and in the more avant-garde wing of establishment theatre. In the last ten years it has been the touring and fringe theatre circuits which have been the main areas of theatrical growth, and it is within these that a range of radical ideas and artistic experiments have flourished. It has been here too that feminist and gay criticisms of male dominance in both the established media and socialist theatre led to the formation of feminist and gay theatre groups, and to a slow recognition that sexual politics is an important political force.

However, theatre does not in or by itself produce theory or claim to lead political organisation. It reflects and transforms theoretical and political knowledge and practice into works of art — even the crudest piece of instrumental agitprop touches on emotional and personal responses in a way that the political pamphlet cannot. In addition, the live immediacy of theatrical performance — producers and consumers taking part together in an event that links art and politics — makes it attractive and rewarding to theatre workers wanting to develop greater artistic and political control of their work.

The Women's Liberation Movement, and the Gay Liberation Front, which started in 1969-70, developed areas of ideological struggle which had their immediate roots in the student movement of 1968. Student protest against local, national and international events developed from some of the contradictory aspects of Western ideology: the benefits of the post-World War II welfare state and the economic booms of the fifties and sixties produced the apparent fulfilment of a liberal ideal of widely available education for the young, accompanied by a new economic independence which was part of objectively rising material standards — the new 'affluence'. Students questioned the gap between aspiration and reality. Education and greater affluence did not bring with them an increased sense of control and participation, and world events in the sixties — the American war in Vietnam, the Soviet invasion of Czechoslovakia — followed the radicalising experiences of the Campaign for Nuclear Disarmament and the rock and counter-culture which formed a focus for new working- and middle-class protest in the previous decade.

The massive pop festivals of the sixties had generated a sense of collective pleasure, a participation in a culture which ran counter to the bland, monolithic cultural fare offered by early fifties popular music and television. From 1968 onwards, a new understanding was beginning to emerge of the importance of the way the dominant ideology was diffused through the arts, media, education and communications of bourgeois society. The problem of the passivity of the consumer-individual took on a new importance, and the importance of culture and the arts in everyday life extended the traditional definitions of political struggle which had largely been focused at the point of production. The counter-culture asserted the importance of ideological struggle, protested at the restricted roles within the professions for which young people were being educated, but ignored an obvious contradiction inside its own ranks. Within both the counter-culture and the student movement, women remained second-class participants. Even the so-called sexual permissiveness of the sixties was dogged by this double standard. Feminism, which had been dormant as a political force for half a century re-emerged from within the student movement in a new way. In June 1969 feminist historian Sheila Rowbotham exposed the hidden oppression within the new left:

> Glance at any Left theoretical journal or go to any large meeting and you won't find many articles either by or about women and you won't see many women speaking. Think of the way women relate to the Left groups. Very largely we complement the men: we hold small groups together, we send out reminders, we type the leaflets, we administer rather than initiate . . . Revolutionary students are quite capable of wolf-whistling and cat-calling when a girl speaks; more common though is tolerant humour, patronising derision or that silence after which everyone continues as if nobody had spoken. — *The Body Politic* (p22)

In spring 1970 the Women's Movement was formed, and in the autumn the Gay Liberation Front began holding meetings. Both movements were dedicated to transforming the social structures which oppress people on the grounds of sexual difference or preference, and both movements quickly focused on the entrenched ideology which underpins the sexual division of labour within the family, in which woman is assumed to be confined by her biological role, and in which the heterosexual imperative is held to be the norm.

The contradictions of affluence in welfare-state society affected women very specifically. While the vote in 1928 had finally granted a degree of political emancipation, and creation of access to education and white-collar and professional jobs had widened career choices, the 'woman's place is in the home' ideology reappeared after World War II. In addition, social change had affected the family more radically than ever in the twentieth century. Increased middle-class affluence produced greater isolation for the middle-class housewife, and the break-up of the extended working-class family imposed its own strains on women. These strains were generally dismissed as individual neuroses, although it is interesting to note that there was a small group of women novelists writing in the late fifties and early sixties (Doris Lessing, Margaret Drabble, Penelope Mortimer, for example) who were beginning to give imaginative voice to some of these strains.

Following the return of the Labour Government in 1964 (after thirteen years of Conservative rule) a number of legislative reforms implicitly recognised that certain restrictions on family and sexual relations could no longer be enforced. In 1967 an Abortion Act and an Act partially legalising male homosexuality were passed (female homosexuality has never been illegal — popular myth has it that when the first anti-homosexual legislation was passed Queen Victoria was so horrified at the mere thought of lesbianism that she refused to believe it could exist . . .). In 1969 the Divorce Reform Act eased conditions for divorce, and in 1970 the Equal Pay Act opened up the possibility of equal pay for men and women becoming a reality by the end of 1975. (In fact women still earn on average about half the amount that men earn.) More efficient contraceptive methods, including the pill, made it more possible for women to separate sex for pleasure from sex for procreation. The potentials for greater freedom of choice for women collided with the ideology of hearth and home — and the fact that it was middle-class women (the most privileged) who protested first, indicates the discrepancy between aspiration and reality which affected women both within and outside the student movement.

At the first Women's Liberation Conference at Ruskin College, Oxford, in spring 1970 four 'demands' were formulated: Equal Pay, Equal Education and Opportunity, 24-Hour Nurseries, and Free Contraception and Abortion on Demand. The demands crystallised the particular character of female oppression, linking woman's position in the paid workforce with her position in the family. The Gay Liberation Front addressed itself to the oppression and discrimination against homosexuals throughout society, putting the major part of their emphasis on the right of homosexuals to be open and explicit about their lifestyles. 'Coming out' as gay, publicly and proudly, was paralleled by the way women (heterosexual and lesbian) were beginning to 'come out' with pride rather than shame as women. Both movements emphasised self-activity, and both aimed to combine struggles against overt prejudice and discrimination with the struggle to overcome an individually internalised view of women and gays as inferior and/or 'unnatural'.

From the very beginnings theatrical self-expression was part of the feminist and gay movements — street theatre protests against the Miss World contests of 1970 and 1971, and events accompanying demonstrations and processions. Until 1973-74 feminist and gay theatre was scattered and sporadic — in addition to women's street theatre, writer Jane Arden produced *Holocaust,* a semi-surreal play about female archetypes in 1971. In 1972 the Women's Street Theatre Group devised 'The Equal Pay Show', a cartoon-like analysis with songs about the limits of the new legislation. Also in 1972 members of the Bolton Octagon Theatre in Education Team wrote *Sweetie Pie,* which took the four demands as its point of departure in investigating the opportunities and restrictions a working-class woman faces in society today. Stylistically the plays ranged over traditional agitprop (a message with a smile and a song), to expressionism (a huge deodorant and a giant penis in one street play), and surrealism. I wrote a play about the Miss World contest which was performed at a London lunchtime theatre in 1972, and writer Pam Gems wrote two monologues for women which were performed at the Almost Free Theatre in early 1973.

The three groups in this book represent three strands of development in socialist/feminist/gay theatre. Red Ladder began as a theatrical adjunct to 'Agitprop', a political/cultural group which was set up in London in 1968 as a left-wing publisher, bookshop, information and advice centre. They were a mixed theatre group, and first conceived their idea of a 'women's' play in 1972. The Women's Theatre Group had some tenuous links with the earlier street theatre group, but came into being in its present form after a season of plays written, directed and stage managed by women at the Almost Free Theatre in the autumn of 1973. Gay Sweatshop was formed in 1975, following a similar season of gay plays (all-male) at the same theatre. Red Ladder has remained a mixed group, developing socialist/feminist elements in parallel; the Women's Theatre Group has been all-female, and Gay Sweatshop has produced plays with a mixed company, and also all-male and all-female plays.

The success of the women's season at the Almost Free drew attention to the position of women in the theatre: prejudice against women as technicians, limited and limiting roles for actresses, women writers and directors in a minority, and very few women in positions of administrative or artistic control. The season also brought together feminists who were attracted to expressing their politics through theatrical work, and professional theatre workers who were dissatisfied with available opportunities.

The gay theatre season two years later introduced gay theatre workers to a new consciousness; 'camp' has long been an element in entertainment, and there has also been a tolerated ghetto of male gayness within theatrical social life. But the new consciousness of gay pride asserted itself not simply as ghetto humour, but as a desire for gay people to represent themselves onstage, without having either to apologise for, or send up, their self-image.

Red Ladder, the Women's Theatre Group and Gay Sweatshop share a number of features: the overall desire to control the form and content of the work, the work method and access to audiences. Red Ladder began as a part-time street theatre group, taking theatre to people in non-theatre venues and contexts. Over the years, their work consolidated, they began to receive an Arts Council subsidy and became fulltime. They built up a careful network of contacts and audiences within the labour movement, and in community groups — such as those on housing estates and women's groups — a process which took several years. Red Ladder (like the other two groups) defines itself as a 'collective', a term and practice which has two important characteristics. Firstly, it enables members of the group to control democratically all aspects of their work, from planning a tour to deciding on set design. Secondly, it implies a challenge to authoritarianism and the rigid division of labour which help perpetuate oppressive relations, and stifle creativity and contributions from performers. It is a form of workers' control in which the touring theatre groups are basically run by performers. The plays in this book (only partially in the case of Gay Sweatshop) were devised, written and directed by the performers themselves. More recently, both Red Ladder and the Women's Theatre Group have begun employing writers, directors and designers for specific projects — but the plays in this book essentially emerge from the early experience of the collective process.

Critics and the conventional media display great suspicion about the value of the collective writing process. It is generally assumed that such an approach cannot produce work of importance or quality — that accolade is reserved for the individual writer, the artist supposedly touched by genius. To defend collective devising is not to deny the importance of the individual artistic voice; but the work done by socialist groups in the last ten years has shown that collective devising at its most effective can represent an intense movement towards a peak of consciousness at a particular historical moment. The need for such plays is thrown up by the way in which the new political ideologies and struggles are becoming public and visible, and the fact that all three plays were by turns provocatively and enthusiastically received proves that they were able to present new and challenging subject matter to audiences who could see the plays as supporting their own experiences, or as challenging to their assumptions.

Whereas Red Ladder's work was situated mainly within the labour movement, the Women's Theatre Group bridged an important gap between the work of groups like Theatre in Education teams — who work all the time within schools — and the touring agitprop groups who seek their audiences largely among adults. This meant that the Women's Theatre Group also built their network of contacts and audiences very carefully, necessitating a familiarity with the ideas and experiences of their audiences. Both Red Ladder and the Women's Theatre Group always followed their plays with discussions, demystifying the gap between performer and audience, and making the political consciousness-raising which followed a performance something which was also shared, thus helping to politicise the theatre-going process itself.

The sense of accountability to their audiences which has characterised the work of all three groups is reflected in the way they often took suggestions for their next play from audiences — as was the case for both *Strike...* and *Care and Control*. Their composition reflected different perspectives on sexual politics: Red Ladder's political base line was a socialist approach, which was then influenced by feminism. The Women's Theatre Group's base line was feminism, which was then influenced by socialism. Gay Sweatshop in its early stages consisted of a mixture of people — some with socialist/feminist awareness, some with a gay pride consciousness and some who were gay but had never previously dared to 'come out' in their theatre work.

In all groups the collective process of control over a product which in itself contained a radical approach to sexual politics, directly affected the working relations within the groups. The Women's Theatre Group were consciously a women-only group, emphasising the feminist principle of women working together independently of male domination, and a commitment to demonstrating in their work the solidarity between women ('sisterhood'). This meant having to face responsibilities which in mixed groups they might avoid — the vexed question of who can and can't lift heavy weights, and facing the surprise of teachers and pupils at the fact that a group of women could organise their own work.

When Red Ladder began to work on *Strike...* they found themselves examining the power relations within the group in a new way. One member, Steve, commented in retrospect:

> It was certainly true that till then the men, and the most articulate men, were dominant in the way the plays were written.

and another, Chris, amplified:

> The significant difference between this and plays we'd done before was that here for the first time there was a kind of meeting point of people's 'personal experience' and the sort of labour movement politics we'd been into previously. It wasn't so much 'on behalf of'; it had much more of ourselves in it.

The Gay Sweatshop play was researched and devised collectively, but when they had assembled the material, they decided to ask me, as a writer, to come in and script the material for them. In their working method on *Care and Control*

Gay Sweatshop used both collective and conventional methods— the play was initiated by the women in the company, but had two male characters (played by the same actor), and was then scripted by an individual. Although the play was conceived of in connection with a specific issue — fighting to help argue for the rights of lesbian mothers in custody cases — it was structured like a conventional theatre piece — with an interval, and not to be followed by discussion.

The form of *Strike...* and *Care and Control* owes a debt both to the conventional and the alternative media. Television has accustomed people to the short play with its predominantly naturalistic form — a slice of apparent 'real life' cutting into the real lives of our individual living rooms. Lunchtime and political theatre (for different functional reasons) also utilise the short play form — the latter because plays are often part of a longer programme and/or are followed by discussions. But what used to be called the 'one-act' play is no longer considered a curio — or only half of the real thing. It has become an accepted form in its own right.

The need to find points of identification with audiences means that this question of form is central. The theatre of the seventies has developed its own styles and uses of realism, and all three plays rest on a bedrock of demonstrable naturalism. Historically, artistic movements which seek to represent the experiences of oppressed groups reach initially for a realistic and immediately recognisable clarity. Thus French realism in journalism and fiction followed the 1848 revolution; in the twenties and thirties the impact of the Bolshevik revolution led to a politicisation of avant-garde art and literature, and to the emergence of a new realism based on the socialist experience. Such realism has a radical impact when the content is new, when the selection of ordinary everyday elements in life are shaped into a work of art.

All three plays in this book rest heavily on the everyday activity and conversation of their subjects— at work, in daily domestic maintenance, in the stuff of conversation and chat between women — too often dismissed as 'trivial gossip'. The naturalism in all three plays shows that women's conversation has political potential, and is the opposite of trivial. However, none of them are simply examples of a new earnest kitchen-sink realism. They all benefit from an input from popular culture, television - entertainment, and art-theatre. Although the fundamental aim behind all three plays is to present realistic works of art which will provoke recognition among their audiences, they do so in ways which continually break through the boundaries of naturalistic story-telling. In this way the plays all have a dynamic which is specific to them as works of theatre, as forms which are entertaining and to some degree alternatives to simple television-naturalism. In each case the realistic elements have a didactic purpose, and this purpose is sharpened by the non-realistic elements, such as music, stylisation, and direct contact with the audience.

Strike... and *My Mother Says*... use songs and strong visual imagery; *Care and Control* gives us naturalistic snatches of three couples' lives in the first half and expands the second half into the stylised and alienating atmosphere of a court hearing. The breaks within the realistic form allow both for more explicit didacticism — as in some of the songs — and for a more subtle, indirect impact made by the entertainment value of the music, or, as in the court scenes, by swift and dynamic juxtaposition.

Because the complex and intricate nature of sexual oppression needs to be fought within and between individuals, as well as through organised political campaigns, the way consciousness of sexual politics is developed through individuals in the plays is important. All agitprop work aims to place the individual within his or her social context, and one of the aims of agitational theatre has been to show the coming to political consciousness of an individual who then becomes an emblem for the possibilities of collective consciousness. In the majority of plays this individual has been a man — one of the few which has a woman as the central character is Brecht's *The Mother* — a play which has been performed often during the seventies. The mother is a paradigm of the most backward individual moving to the most advanced state of socialist consciousness, and Red Ladder consciously used the play both as a structural model for *Strike*..., and also as a model for one of the play's central messages — a woman's journey into political consciousness.

However, the way the politics are expressed through the central female character is very different in the two plays. The importance of Brecht's mother lies in the way she comes to represent a generalised male-defined working-class consciousness, rather than in her presence as a woman whose experience is important for its own sake. From being a semi-lumpen, illiterate woman, outside economic production, she joins the peasants and workers (mainly men) in their struggle. Her social position as a woman (and 'mother') enables her to portray humane and caring qualities, but her political education consists of her joining an already defined struggle. Her femaleness is only important insofar as it gives socialism a caring face, and the implication is that class consciousness is a one-way struggle: from simple backwardness to simple progressiveness. implicitly Brecht's play (potent as it is in its own terms) echoes a crude interpretation of the traditional economistic Marxist assumption that 'The first premise for the emancipation of women is the reintroduction of the entire female sex into public industry'. (Engels, *Origin of the Family, Private Property, and the State*)

With the impact of a feminism which goes beyond such traditional assumptions, Red Ladder attempts to show that an awareness of the oppression of women leads to a two-way struggle. The women learn to fight within their union at work, but Helen, the central character also initiates a complementary struggle in her own home. While women learn to participate and affect male-dominated areas of life (work, the union), a counter-demand is made of men: that they be prepared to share equally in housework and looking after their children. The changes in Dave's consciousness as a man and husband are presented as an inevitable corollary to Helen's changing situation. The play tackles the basic division of labour in the home, in a combinaton of bold visual imagery and humour which, while not selling short the real conflicts between men and women, aims at the ultimate strategy of a class solidarity shared by men and women. Although the main emphasis in the play is on the women's self-activity, the end suggests the possibility of an alliance between men and women, in which the divide and rule ideology of bourgeois social relations has been exposed.

My Mother Says... takes a consciously partisan pro-women perspective. The play focuses on the feelings and roles of the women and girls vis-à-vis sexual expectations, but without emerging in any way as a crude anti-men piece. In showing the various conflicting attitudes to sexuality among the women, the play outlines women's relationship to bourgeois sexual morality and their attempts to develop choices for themselves: the embarrassed woman teacher trying to teach girls 'facts of life' they already know is contrasted with the gleeful Gran who liked sex and isn't ashamed to say so, and the anxious, moral mother who is little help to her teenage daughter.

Both plays are about heterosexual experience — that of the majority. *Care and Control,* though it began as an 'issue' play (about the problems of lesbian mothers in custody cases) ended up raising some searching questions about the dominant assumptions behind family life in order to maintain the status quo of a family pattern which assumes heterosexual, monogamous woman at its centre. When women transgress this norm, the law will try to make them toe the line. The play shows how such 'transgression' can range from a mother who chooses a lesbian relationship to a mother who simply wants to live on her own with her child. Again, the emphasis is mainly on the female experience. The two male characters are little more than ciphers in the play as it stands — the male experience is the least developed area in the play. Unlike the other two plays, the central message does not emerge via an individual consciousness, but rather through the interplay of the two halves — the impersonal state machine and the personal, individual life, showing the clash between the subtleties of lived experience, and the rigidity of the dominant ideology.

The three plays approach the same object from different and complementary angles: *Strike*... delineates the contradictory workings of sexism among working people whose class interests are the same; the play demonstrates the absolutely intertwined relationship between change in the family and change at the point of production. It also locates trade union struggle (with its own internal contradictions) as a necessary instrument for political change. *My Mother Says...* focuses on an earlier stage of social experience — young women who have not yet fully entered the adult world. Terri and Wendy might be teenage versions of Helen, being prepared for the contradictions of adult womanhood. The play suggests the links between women's approach to their sexuality, pleasure and reproduction and the wider choices women can make in their lives as adults. *Care and Control* explores the contradiction between the real, lived dilemmas of motherhood and the pressures of the capitalist state.

The overall objective of the plays is to contribute to the socialist feminist intervention in today's world; this involves bringing theatre into the lives of ordinary people, and bringing political struggle into the world of theatre work. Sexual politics along with the class-conscious political theatre movement have affected the established theatre and the other media — both negatively and positively. Women writers (feminist and non-feminist) are now viewed with a mixture of interest and suspicion; actresses in established theatre companies are protesting more vigorously about having fewer and less interesting roles than actors; gradually women are invading the traditional male strongholds of technical and stage management work. The advances are small, but they would have been impossible without the political presence of gay and feminist consciousness permeating the relatively autonomous area of fringe/political theatre. It is only relatively autonomous, since the material conditions under which it is produced and consumed are still those of bourgeois society; its strength and importance lies in what it represents as a form of struggle within cultural production. Live theatre may only draw a minority audience, compared to film and TV, but it is its statistical marginality which gives its workers greater mobility and freedom for experimentation and some degree of control over their work.

The intellectual left has given far more attention to the mass distributed arts than it has to theatre; rightly in terms of analysing what is beamed out to large numbers of people by the dominant culture. But theatre must not be dismissed simply on statistical grounds. The fact that theatre is still a labour intensive medium, the fact that there is live contact between producers and consumers, the fact that political theatre can with great assurance seek out new audiences, and the fact that drama is being used more and more as an educational medium, makes it a vital area for cultural struggle.

However, theatre has the disadvantage that performance is ephemeral as an artefact. Films and books continue to be circulated and read; in Britain almost the only plays published are those by writers who have already achieved some success. Both commercial and feminist presses rejected this book; largely on the grounds that it 'wouldn't sell'. Such a view not only underestimates the value of the play, but also its audience. These plays can be read as social documentary, they can be performed by other groups, or they can act as inspiration for groups and/or individuals to make their own plays. Published literature is starved of work which explores contemporary experience, and which presents women and gays with real interest and/or sympathy. It would be a pleasure to be able to say that both the form and content of these plays are dated. But they are not. Ten years is a short time in which to challenge centuries of tradition in theatre. This book is only a small part of that ongoing challenge. I hope other publishers will be encouraged to follow its example.

Michelene Wandor

STRIKE WHILE THE IRON IS HOT
Red Ladder Theatre

Red Ladder first decided to make a 'Women's Play' in 1972. The impetus to do so came from two directions: from the women inside the company whose growing involvement with the Women's Liberation Movement had made them want a play that was more closely related to their own lives than issue-based plays on rents or industrial relations; and from the Labour Movement, which Red Ladder was firmly rooted in by this time, who wanted a play that raised the questions of equal pay, and job opportunity discrimination to feed into the developing campaign to implement the Equal Pay Act.

Initially the play was conceived as one of several 'units': a collection of fifteen-minute theatre pieces on a wide range of subjects — the uses of technology, housing, Ireland, racism etc . . . women(!). The idea was that a 'unit' would be selected that was suitable for a given meeting/audience — for example the housing unit for a tenants' audience — but in addition, one or two other units would be performed on the same occasion to broaden the horizons of the evening and deepen the politics discussed. The 'units' could also be performed individually at strike meetings or during dinner breaks in canteens where time was at a premium. Initially, then, the women's play was conceived as one of a number of tools for discussion.

Predictably we couldn't keep the 'unit' length down to fifteen minutes. The first two — on the Housing Finance Act and the implications of new technology for white collar workers — ran to thirty and forty minutes respectively and were only ever twice performed in the same evening. The third of these new units was the Women's Play. That it should have been relegated to third place was pointed to by the women in Red Ladder as symptomatic of its priority for Red Ladder men. By the time the first units were on the road, however, a first draft of the Women's Play was under discussion in the company (spring 1973).

The problem of the first draft was felt to be that it was too factory and trade union oriented at the expense of the home. For the developing sexual politics of the company it seemed to 'deal' too much with 'issues' and didn't delve sufficiently deeply into the causes of sexual oppression. Nor did it adequately explore the relationships between men and women. So this draft was scrapped and it was not until the autumn of 1973 that the project was begun again. This time the whole company threw itself into two months of reading, discussion and interviewing. In these talks the two directions of origin of the play — the inner and the outer — confronted each other. And the division was not always along sexual lines. Some of us stuck rigidly to our particular versions of Marx,

Lenin and dialectical materialism: for this 'side' of the argument the key to understanding and ending the oppression of women lay in first ending the exploitation of the working class by the 'bourgeoisie'. Others of us were more interested in what Shulamith Firestone had to say: for this 'side' the roots of women's oppression lay in the age-old domination of women by men; the oppression of one class by another was of secondary importance in history to the oppression of women by men — patriarchy. In the end these extreme positions softened towards each other and a central position was taken by the company which gave equal importance to both arguments. Our view was summed up in two banners which appeared simultaneously at the end of the play. They read: 'Women will never be free while workers are in chains' and 'Workers will never be free while women are in chains'.

The importance that these discussions held for us was reflected in a scene which was originally Scene Two. It was a stylised 'History of the Family' from Paleolithic times to the present day. It attempted to show that the family has not always been the nuclear family that we know today but that it has changed with history. Eventually the scene was dropped. Its deliberate didacticism was felt to be too out of character with the narrative realism (also stylised) of the rest of the play. It was a case of 'get-it-all-in-ism': political correctness in conflict with dramatic effectiveness.

Preliminary work on the play brought together personal experience, theory, and understanding more about the lives of working class women through talking with 'contacts' and friends. It provided the foundation upon which the play was then made.

The playmaking stage was undertaken by four of the company of nine — three women and one man. Their drafts and outlines came repeatedly back to the company for comment and modification. The play was scripted by late January 1974 when it went into rehearsal and underwent further script changes. It was first performed at an AUEW TASS weekend school at Weston-Super-Mare on March 11th 1974.

A Woman's Work is Never Done or *Strike While the Iron is Hot* as it was also called, was an immediate success. In the next two years it was performed at trade union meetings, weekend schools, tenants, associations, women's liberation meetings, women's groups, mothers' groups, in working mens' clubs, schools and colleges all over the country.

The play was made to be followed by a discussion. The scene that almost invariably provided most comment was the abortion scene. In making the play we had argued about the sensitivity of such a scene: would it alienate our audiences: was it too risky? No. We would definitely include it. But we were still asked on occasions to cut it for certain audiences. Glasgow was one instance where organisers felt that a largely Catholic audience might be turned against the play as a whole, and more dangerously(!) the sponsoring organisation (the Labour Party) by the inclusion of such controversy. In the event we refused to cut it and our audiences were not so shocked as to reject either the play as a whole or the sequence on abortion — even if many of them might have disagreed with it. We also played to an audience of 900 in Liberty Hall in Dublin: the scene prompted a handful of walkouts but the play gained a standing ovation.

In 1975, the National Union of Public Employees organised a tour of the play for their membership on Tyneside. But they wanted the play to have a more tangible relevance to what was going on in the union in the area at the time. So one of us went to Newcastle in advance to research and write a new scene to replace Scene Three. Helen would now get a job as a school-meals cook instead of seamstress in a sweatshop. This relatively small change gave the play a specific point of reference which tied it into a contemporary NUPE dispute.

Originally the play only had one song — at the end. But gradually more songs were brought in: written in the company and commissioned or taken ready made from outside songwriters — Sandra Kerr, Ron and Leon Rosselson. The introduction of more songs in the course of the play's touring was a response to its changing context of performance. In the opening few months of performance it was seen primarily by audiences of trade unionists, students and feminists who were gathered together, in spite of our play, to talk about issues the play dwelt on: the function of the play was to enhance rather than initiate thought and discussion about its subject. Consequently the play did not have to stand alone as entertainment for non-politically conscious audiences, even though it had been designed to do so. But as we got further into the tour, the popular appeal of the play became increasingly apparent: it seemed to give anyone and everyone a way through to animated involvement with what it was about. So we began to broaden our audiences. And with this broadening the context of performance shifted: now we were being asked to provide an evening's entertainment with discussion in a working men's club or at a social, in addition to the earlier more directly political contexts. So we introduced more songs to strengthen the play's broadening appeal and enrich the rhythms of the audience's involvement. We felt we needed slightly less of a stark play and a bit more of a show. With these additions the play grew from fifty to eighty minutes. Red Ladder performed *Strike While the Iron is Hot* in various versions until April 1976. By this time it had had about 200 performances to about 20,000 people. The version here is the one we ended up with.

Chris Rawlence

Strike While the Iron is Hot was first performed at an AUEW TASS weekend school at Weston-Super-Mare on March 11, 1974.

CAST

Most of the performers play more than one character:

Female 1:   HELEN
Female 2:   BRIDE'S MOTHER
             CHRISSIE
             Singer of 'The Maintenance Engineer'
             DORIS (Mrs Taylor)
             CANTEEN WORKER
Female 3:   GROOM'S MOTHER
             IRIS
             MRS EDWARDS
             MARY
             SHEILA
Male 1:   DAVE
             One of Council characters
Male 2:   VICAR
             BEST MAN
             Shop Steward (GEORGE)
             One of Council characters
             JOB EVALUATOR
             EDDIE
Male 3:   BRIDE'S FATHER
             MIKE
             Trade union official (JOHN)

Other small parts are played by members of the cast as available.

Strike While the Iron is Hot was made by Marian Sedley, Richard Seyd, Noreen MacDowell, Carlos Guarita, Chris Rawlence, Steve Trafford, Glen Park, Richard Stourac and Kathleen McCreery. In its two years of touring the following also performed in it: Susan Glanville, Judy Lloyd, Diana Quick, Malcolm Reid, Libby Mason.

Don't Get Married, Girls by Leon Rosselson

Don't get married, girls
You'll sign away your life.
You may start off as a woman
But you'll end up as a wife.
You could be a vestal virgin,
Take the veil and be a nun,
But don't get married, girls,
For marriage isn't fun.

Oh, it's fine when you're romancing and he plays the lover's part,
You're the roses in his garden, you're the flame that warms his heart.
And his love will last for ever and he'll promise you the moon,
But just wait until you're wedded and he'll sing a different tune.
You're his tapioca pudding, you're the dumplings in his stew,
And he'll soon begin to wonder what he ever saw in you.
Still he takes without complaining all the dishes you provide,
But you see he has to have his bit of jam tart on the side.

So don't get married, girls, it's very badly paid,
You may start off as the mistress but you'll end up as the maid.
Be a daring deep-sea diver, be a polished polyglot.
But don't get married, girls, for marriage is a plot.

Have you seen him in the morning with a face that looks like death,
He's got dandruff on his pillow and tobacco on his breath,
And he wants some reassurance with his cup of tea in bed,
'Cos he's got worries with the mortgage and the bald patch on his head.
So you try to boost his ego, iron his shirt and warm his vest,
Then you get him off to work, the mighty hunter is restored,
And he leaves you there with nothing but the dreams you can't afford.

So don't get married, girls, for men are all the same,
They just use you when they need you, you'd do better on the game.
Be a call-girl, be a stripper, be a hostess, be a whore,
But don't get married girls 'cos then you'll be all four.

When he comes home in the evening he can hardly spare a look,
All he says is 'What's for dinner?' After all, you're just the cook,
But when he takes you to a party, he eyes you with a frown,

And you know you've got to look your best, you mustn't let him down,
And he'll clutch you with that 'look what I've got' sparkle in his eyes,
Like he's entered for a raffle and he's won you for the prize,
But when the party's over, you'll be slogging through the sludge,
Half the time a decoration and the other half a drudge.

So don't get married, it'll drive you round the bend,
It's the lane without a turning, it's the end without an end.
Change your lover every Friday, take up tennis, be a nurse,
But don't get married, girls, for marriage is a curse.

ACT ONE

The show was performed with six rostra and the bare essentials of lighting. There was no set: the bed scene, for example, was performed on elevated rostrum using a bedspread. In addition to the rostra we used the red step-ladder, several beer crates and a small table. Musical accompaniment to the songs was as simple as possible — usually a guitar and sometimes a trumpet as well. A tape was used for effects — eg, the Wedding March — when needed. Costume changes took place each side of the rostra within sight of the audience.

Scene One

The wedding. HELEN — *the bride* — *her* MOTHER, *her* FATHER, DAVE — *the groom* — *his* MOTHER, *the* BEST MAN, *enter to the Wedding March. The* VICAR *appears at the top of the red ladder.*

VICAR   Who giveth this woman to be married to this man?

BRIDE'S FATHER   I do.

VICAR   Wilt thou have this woman to be thy lawful wedded wife? Wilt thou love her and keep her, honour her and comfort her, in sickness and in health and, forsaking all others, keep thee only unto her for as long as ye both shall live?

GROOM'S MOTHER   You've got a responsibility now, Dave. Make her a good home for the kids, like your Dad did for me and she won't mind who wears the trousers.

GROOM   I will.

VICAR   Wilt thou have this man to be thy lawful wedded husband? Wilt thou love, honour and obey him and, forsaking all others, keep thee only unto him for as long as ye both shall live?

BRIDE'S MOTHER   I've always found that if you look after a man properly he'll look after you. It's the little things that count — having his dinner ready when he comes home and his slippers out. Make him feel appreciated, like he's the man in the house.

BRIDE   I will.

VICAR   I now pronounce you man and wife. (*He exits*)

Wedding March. Confetti throwing and general congratulatory chat, turns into reception.

BEST MAN   Alright, let's have a bit of hush. Quiet, please, quiet, please. There's going to be a speech from the bride's father. Quiet, please. Ssh.

BRIDE'S FATHER   Well, I'm not accustomed to making public speeches, but I can remember a time when our Helen here, were a little girl, and I made her a doll's house with my own hands.

BRIDE'S MOTHER   Eee, that's right, he did.

BRIDE'S FATHER   Well, it seems like only yesterday. And to think now she's going to be getting a home of her own.

GROOM   With a bit of luck, eh?

BRIDE'S FATHER   Yes, well, I'd just like to say, I hope all your troubles are little ones.

BRIDE'S MOTHER   Oh, I think it's lovely. (*She weeps*) I can't believe it's my little girl.

BRIDE'S FATHER   Now, now. (*He comforts her*)

GROOM'S MOTHER   The Best Man. Where's the Best Man? Dave, where's the Best Man?

GROOM   John, where are you, John? Where is he?

John is caught, back to audience with his own arms round his neck in the 'snogging gag'.

BRIDE'S MOTHER   Oooh, there he is. I think it's disgusting.

GROOM   Come on out of it, will you, John.

BEST MAN   Yeh, well, sorry about that. Well, I'm sure you'll all like to join with me congratulating Dave here on getting himself such a lovely little wife, eh? But you know, I can remember the time when Dave and Helen first met.

GROOM   Er now, steady on, John.

BEST MAN   It was down the dance hall, wasn't it? We were sitting there and we seen Helen coming towards us across the dance floor. I turned to Dave and I says, 'Hey up', and you know, before I know it, he was there. Well, given half a chance, I'd be standing there meself today.

BRIDE'S MOTHER   Ooh, I am glad he isn't.

BRIDE'S FATHER   Huh.

GROOM   Yes. Thanks. Well, I always think of that as the one time the Best Man didn't win.

General applause and polite laughter.

BEST MAN   Right, then, couple of photographs, cut the cake.

A cardboard cake is erected: the BEST MAN *directs all into a photographic pose around it.*

BEST MAN   Alright, everybody, close together now.

They make a 'group' around the cake.

BEST MAN   Hold it.

Flash. Everybody freezes into a photograph except —

GROOM (*to the audience*)   Helen's a real good looker, and bright too, for a woman. She listens to me, makes me feel appreciated and she's always saying 'You're the boss, Dave.' I mean, what more could you want? Eh?

BEST MAN   Lovely. Right, another one from over here.

Another 'group' is made.

BEST MAN   Hold it.

Everybody freezes into a photograph except —

HELEN (*to the audience*)   It's a big step, but I know I'm doing the right thing. Dave and I were meant for each other. All I've ever wanted is to marry him and have his kids.

BEST MAN   Lovely.

Everyone moves round the bride to congratulate her. Out of this mêlée steps the GROOM'S MUM.

GROOM'S MUM (*to the audience*)   'Ere, you should see their presents: tea-sets, coffee pots, hoovers, sheets. Well, anyone could make a good home if they had all those.

She rejoins the mêlée. HELEN *is hidden by the group. Exclamations about the beautiful presents. Out of this comes the sound of wedding bells. All the characters except* HELEN *exit leaving her standing there, with a broom in her hand, still in her wedding dress. She starts to sweep up the confetti and the wedding bells fade into the introductory music to 'I Feel Happy'.*

HELEN *sings*   I feel happy
                I'm so lucky
                I feel lovely and sexy and great

> 'Cos I've married
> The most fabulous man —
> I can't wait.

Enter the two MUMS.

MUMS *sing*   Well, that's that, then
> Lovely wedding
> It's the happiest day of your life
> Is she too young?
> Oh, she'll manage,
> She'll make a good wife.

They exit. Wedding bells. Placard: 'And they lived happily ever after', which is then turned over to show: 'The End'. The rest of the cast, visible but offstage continue the song.

CHORUS   You've got to hang out the clothes today
> Likely to rain
> You've got to put the dinner on
> Go to the shops
> Got to wash the pots
> Got to make the beds
> Got to scrub the floor
> Hallo — need a cup of tea
> Need a cup of tea

'Need a cup of tea' develops to a crescendo; underneath it available members of the cast start an argument as between two children.

HELEN   What's up? What's the matter? Will you stop fighting, you two. Let him play with it. Little devils. I've been up half the night with our Peter. He woke his Dad up an' all. Dave was furious. Still, you can understand it, can't you? He's got a hard day's work ahead of *him*.

CHILD (*from visible cast offstage*)   Can I have a biscuit, Mum?

HELEN   Oh, not before tea, love. Always pestering you for something, aren't they? Now Elsie next door, she sends hers to a baby minder, while she's out at work, like. I don't know, though. I think a little kiddie needs its mother's love, don't you?

CHILD   Look, Mum.

HELEN   Hey, you, get off that floor. I've just scrubbed it. Oh, get outside, I'm sick of the sight of you.

CHORUS   She's a mother
Twice over
She's been breeding and feeding and washing the nappies and wiping their bottoms and getting their meals,
And she doesn't feel
Quite as pretty as she used to feel.

HELEN   The trouble with being stuck at home all day — it's boring. I mean, all I can do is go next door and say 'Hello, I've just scrubbed my floor', and she'll say 'Oh, have you? I just cleaned my windows'. I mean, who wants to know? It's not just housework that's boring — it's me. Eh, I wonder if Elsie'd baby-sit tonight. Well, even if it was just for an hour we could go down to the pub. Oh, but then it would be Dave and his mates talking about cars and factory, and union and politics. Like I said, who wants to know that I've just washed my floor. Still, anything'd be better than being stuck in watching tele again.

CHORUS   She feels pretty
Pretty boring
She's been washing and cooking and cleaning and scrubbing and ironing and shopping and wiping and drying, and breeding and feeding — she's been had,
Being a housewife
Is enough to drive anyone mad.

The cast, visible offstage, share the following lines between them, rising to a climax as they direct them at HELEN.

GROOM'S MUM   Anyone can make a good home if they had all those.

BRIDE'S FATHER   I hope all your troubles are little ones.

BRIDE'S MUM   Have his dinner ready when he comes home.

BEST MAN   Dave's got himself a lovely little wife.

HELEN *does a silent scream. This is broken by the groom,* DAVE.

DAVE   Hello, love. I'm home.

HELEN (*tidies herself, puts on 'welcome home' face*)   Hello.

———

Scene Two

Placard: 'A woman's work is never done'. HELEN *and* DAVE*'s sitting-room.* HELEN *is downstage right, ironing.* DAVE *is seated upstage left, reading the* Daily Mirror.

HELEN   Dinner alright, love.

DAVE   Yes. Wouldn't mind a cuppa, though.

HELEN   Alright, Dave.

DAVE   Yes.

HELEN   Elsie said she'd baby-sit so we could go out tonight.

DAVE   Not tonight, love.

HELEN   But there's a good picture on.

DAVE   I'm too tired, love, really.

HELEN   Oh, I'm sick of being stuck here all day. I want to get out.

DAVE   Well, I'm sick to death of going out to work all the time. I want to stay in. Come on, Helen, what's the matter. (*She sits on his knee*)

HELEN   Oh, you never want to go out these days.

DAVE   I just want to stay in and put my feet up.

HELEN   Yes, but it's the same every night. You come home, you get stuck in that chair. If the house fell down you'd still be sat there reading the paper, wouldn't you? Oh, come on, Dave, just for an hour. We could go down to the pub.

DAVE   No.

HELEN   Well, what about tomorrow night then?

DAVE   Oh, I can't manage tomorrow night, love. I've got a union meeting.

HELEN   Oh, it's alright, isn't it? You can go to the union but you can't go out with me.

DAVE   It's different. It's work, the union.

HELEN   It's a night out with the lads.

DAVE   It's not a flaming night out with the lads.

HELEN   Then why do you come home drunk every time? Unions!

DAVE   Look, Helen. Take last week. Old Bill Smedley.

HELEN   Oh, here we go.

DAVE   Now you know him. He's a nice bloke, got a wife and two kids. Now the manager had threatened to give him the sack. That could have been any one of us, Helen, could have been me. The union? — Up there like a shot. Got him his job back in no time. So I'll not have you knocking the union. We'd be a damn sight worse off without them.

HELEN   We couldn't be much worse off than we are right now. Hey, Dave, when are you going to give me that extra two quid on the housekeeping.

DAVE   Two quid? What do you think I am? The Bank of England? You can manage on what you've got.

HELEN   How can I manage on what I've got? Prices are going up, you know. My money doesn't stretch.

DAVE   You don't have to tell me that. I've got all the bills to pay. Bloody rates have just gone up again. Only leaves me four quid by the end of the week.

HELEN   Four quid? And what do you do with that, then?

DAVE   Well, I've a right to the odd pint or two. I work bloody hard for it.

HELEN   And I don't work, I suppose.

DAVE   I'm talking about work, Helen. Down the factory. You should try it sometime.

HELEN   I wouldn't mind. I'm sick and tired of scrimping and saving to get by on your wage.

DAVE   That's gratitude for you. Alright, go on, get yourself a job. You'll soon find out it isn't so bloody marvellous. (*He exits*)

HELEN   Well, at least it would be a change from all this.

HELEN (*sings*)   Is this what married life is meant to be?
Is this what they mean by security?
This never-ending, back-bending drudgery.

There is need, there is love, there's the tenderness
But what happened to the dream of togetherness?
From where came despair and this emptiness?

Isolated and alone, but your time is not your own,
Caring always for another, as a wife, and then a mother,
Always ready, always willing, but it's others do the living.

Must I always live my life through someone else?

It's a prison not a home that I'm living in
As long as I'm confined, I know I'm giving in.
There's a world outside where other things are happening
Your family's at stake — but I've got to make the break.

Will you manage, will you cope

Then the door is open wide
Take a breath and step outside

And if I can do it — why not do it now?

———

Scene Three

> *Placard: 'The Sweatshop'.* PHILIPPE, *the foreman, is supervising* DORIS *and* HELEN *as they sew.* MANAGERESS *enters.*

MANAGERESS Ah, Philippe.

FOREMAN Ah, good morning, madam.

MANAGERESS Lovely day. Now, have the evening dresses arrived?

FOREMAN Er, yes, madam.

MANAGERESS Oh, good. And the representative from Bras for Mamas is calling at eleven o'clock this morning. Ummmm, Lady Feather's just been on the phone. She'd like her dress delivered immediately.

FOREMAN Well, I'm afraid it won't be ready till this afternoon.

MANAGERESS It should have been ready yesterday.

FOREMAN Yes, we've been very busy, and one of the girls has just had a couple of days orf.

MANAGERESS Orf? There's too many people taking time orf . . .

FOREMAN Well, she's usually very reliable.

MANAGERESS I will not tolerate this slapdash approach to the work. If you can't keep those girls under control, I'll have to find somebody who can. (*She climbs the ladder*)

———

Scene Three (a)

DORIS Oh, drat this needle. I think they're making the holes in these things smaller these days.

HELEN Here, Doris, let me do it for you.

DORIS Oh, it's the light in here. It's terrible bad.

HELEN If Sheila misses another day, we won't get this dress done in time.

DORIS Ay, and if we don't, he'll blame me for it. He's always blaming me. I'm always getting the rough end of it, but I'm as good as you young ones any day.

> *Enter* SHEILA.

SHEILA Hello.

DORIS Hey, what's up.

SHEILA   Oh, my youngest's got chicken pox. You should see him. He looks like a currant pudding.

DORIS   Is he better?

SHEILA   No, it goes on for weeks.

HELEN   Who's looking after him today, then?

SHEILA   My mum today and tomorrow, but I don't know what I'm going to do after that. And he didn't want me to come today, either. He screamed. What can you do, eh? Hey, have you been busy.

DORIS   Oh, snowed under.

SHEILA   Oh, I'm ever so sorry.

DORIS   Oh, don't worry, it's not your fault. You couldn't be expected to come in if your kids . . .

FOREMAN   Ah, so you've finally decided to put in an appearance. Aren't *we* the honoured ones. Well?

SHEILA   Oh, I'm sorry, Mr Philippe, I had to take a couple of days off, my kid's sick, you see, and I had to look after him . . .

FOREMAN   Yes, well, there's too many people taking time orf round here; it's not good enough . . .

SHEILA   I'm sorry . . .

FOREMAN   It's slapdash. I'll tell you what you can do. You can go straight down to the cashier's office and collect your cards.

SHEILA   What?

FOREMAN   We don't need your unreliable sort here. (*He exits*)

SHEILA   He didn't want to know about my kid.

HELEN   It's not your fault your little boy's ill. She shouldn't have got the sack for that.

SHEILA   How am I going to manage now? What's Ron going to say?

HELEN   I don't think we should just let him trample all over her like that, Doris.

DORIS   There's nothing you can do. Might as well go home, love. It happens all the time. If you need anything, anything at all, you know where I live.

SHEILA   You'd think it was a crime to have kids. (*She exits*)

HELEN   Well, I don't think it's fair. Well, it could happen to any one of us next. I'll tell you what I'll do. I'll go and see the manageress. Well, she's a woman. She should — understand.

DORIS   You're biting off more than you can chew, love.

———

Scene Three (b)

MANAGERESS (*on the phone*) Oh, Ingrid. How many times have I told you not to ring me at work. What? What? Really, these foreign au pairs, you can't hear a word they're saying. Um, Johnny's ill? Oh. Well, send for Doctor Perkins immediately. Tell him to come round, will you? Okay. 'Bye.

HELEN *knocks*

Come in.

HELEN *enters*

Oh, what do you want?

HELEN Oh, I'm sorry to disturb you, madam . . .

MANAGERESS Well, I am very busy. What is it?

HELEN They've sacked Mrs Brown.

MANAGERESS Mmmmmm?

HELEN Well, I don't think it's fair. You see, her little boy was ill so she couldn't come to work and . . . I've got children, I expect you have as well . . .

MANAGERESS My dear woman, we are in business to provide a reliable service to our customers, and if we don't do that we'll soon go out of business. Then none of us would have jobs to go to, would we? I'm sorry. I can't let my staff take days off when they want to.

HELEN What else could she do? The least you could let her do would be to have two days off to look after her sick child. She's worked for you for over a year, for very low wages . . .

MANAGERESS How dare you be so rude. If you're dissatisfied with your wages, I suggest you find employment elsewhere. That's all.

HELEN Sorry.

HELEN *returns to sew.*

Well, I don't think we should let her get away with it. She threatened me with the sack just for arguing with her.

DORIS Leave it alone, love. You've already gone getting yourself into trouble and that won't help her get her job back, will it.

HELEN Where my husband works, the union would stop them doing things like that.

DORIS Union? They don't care about women. Especially in small places like this.

HELEN   Well, if they don't, they damn well should.

DORIS *exits.*

———

This is an alternative Scene Three written at the request of the National Union of Public Employees on Tyneside for performance as part of the play on a tour of the region in 1975. NUPE organise school meals workers and a number of the shows on that tour were for NUPE branches.

Scene Three

Placard: 'The Working Mum'. A school kitchen. HELEN. IRIS *and* DORIS *are peeling, eyeing and cutting potatoes.*

DORIS   Here, Iris, are the clips on that boiler still dickey?

IRIS   Why, what's up with it?

HELEN   It's tied up with string at the moment. There's boiling water all over the place.

DORIS   Who's doing the custard today?

HELEN   Me.

DORIS   Well, watch yourself. You get too close to it, it'll have you.

Enter EDDIE *struggling with a sack of spuds.*

IRIS   Heyup, here he comes. The fastest sack of potatoes in the North.

HELEN   Oh, he's all muscle, that one, isn't he.

EDDIE   Where shall I put it, girls?

DORIS   Shall we tell him?

EDDIE   You can laugh, but you'd be stuck without a man about the place, eh. (*To audience — coughs and nearly collapses under the weight of the sack as he puts it down*)

Exit EDDIE. IRIS *picks up the sack easily and moves it.*

DORIS   We've got till ten o'clock to get through this lot.

IRIS   It'll be worse next week. You'll be one short.

HELEN   Why? Are you going?

IRIS   My Frank's been made redundant.

DORIS   What? After that big strike?

IRIS   And he can't draw his Social while I'm earning. We get less with me still working, see.

DORIS   Ay, it's a mug's game, isn't it? You end up working for nothing.

HELEN   That's what I keep telling my Dave. You get involved in the union, it brings you nothing but trouble.

DORIS   They were only trying to keep their jobs, you know.

IRIS   Yes. If it hadn't been for the union, they wouldn't even have got their lay-off pay.

DORIS   It's about time you filled in your union form here, Helen, love, you never know when you might need it.

A 'Council' figure appears up the ladder, from behind an umbrella which has 'Council' written on it. Two additional 'Council' figures join him and sing to the tune of 'The Leader of the King's Navee'.

SONG   This is the Civic Centre at your beck and call
We're here to help with anything at all
And even though it takes a month or two
We're always glad to do our best for you.

We'll solve your problems eventually
We'll pull our fingers out for the community.
Your canteen boiler is in need of spares
But there's no money left to pay for any repairs.

So do tell the cooks to be on the alert
It's their own silly fault if one of them gets hurt
We'll fix your boiler eventually
It's all part of helping the community.

Your Labour government has made it clear
The cuts in social services must be severe
The council's down to its last few bob
We really can't afford to keep providing jobs.

The cuts must be of such severity
We'll get no thanks from the community.
This scheme I've invented is an absolute gem —
When jobs fall free, don't fill them up again.

And as for the others who are left to slave,
We'll offer them a bonus scheme to make them brave.
We'll cut our wages bill drastically
And sod the effect on the community.

HELEN (*to the audience*) Well, that bonus scheme sounded alright to us. So after Iris left, we decided to give it a try. Doris were dead against it, mind. But we thought, a bit more money for a bit more work — fair enough.

CHORUS (*to the tune of George Formby's 'When I'm Cleaning Winders'*)

Eye and peel and cut and chop
Bash them spuds and never stop
By half past ten you're fit to drop
When you peel potatoes.

The song accelerates to speed up the women as they work. HELEN *slips while getting a fresh pile of potatoes.*

DORIS Watch it, love. You'll have them all over you in a minute.

HELEN Well, I was trying to get them done on time.

DORIS It's your bonus scheme, love. You asked for it.

CHORUS Eye and peel and cut and chop. (*Verse is repeated and accelerated as the women work on. A scream — the chorus stops —* HELEN *has cut herself*)

DORIS Hey, let's have a look then.

HELEN We can't go on like this. It's bloody dangerous.

Enter the school meals manageress.

DORIS Mrs Taylor's cut herself, Mrs Edwards.

MRS EDWARDS Oh, it's just a scratch. I'll deal with it, Mrs Taylor.

DORIS But I think she should have it seen to, Mrs Edwards.

MRS EDWARDS It can wait. It's only a scratch. Please get on with your work.

DORIS I think we should take her down to the hospital. She needs an injection. It might go bad.

MRS EDWARDS Mrs Taylor, I said it can wait. (*She exits*)

The other women freeze.

HELEN (*to the audience*) Doris were fantastic. She called a meeting there and then. The girls were a bit frightened at first. Disobeying Mrs Edwards, like. But they'd been slipping and sliding all over that kitchen the whole week, we were that hard pushed. They were worried they'd have an accident too, you see. And those clips for the boiler hadn't arrived either.

DORIS (*addressing a kitchen meeting*) Now look, girls, either we go on and chop all our bloody fingers off, or we stop here and now, till we get a promise of extra staff.

HELEN Yes, but —

DORIS   Yes, I know, we voted this bonus scheme in. Well, we can vote it out.

HELEN (*to the audience*) Well, we had a stoppage there and then. We weren't half scared. I mean, there'd be all hell to pay if them meals weren't ready on time. You should have seen the panic.

Urgent confab between MRS EDWARDS *and* COUNCIL OFFICIAL

Phone calls to the civic — the union bloke, he came down to talk to us. He said we should stick it out. So we did. And it worked. We all stood together, you see, and there was nothing they could do about it. We had an extra girl by the end of the week.

I went up the hospital and it weren't too bad. But if it had been worse, Doris said I wouldn't have no protection because I wasn't in the union. Well, after that I filled in the form. It couldn't do any harm.

Mind you, I got the sack a few months later for taking time off work. Of course, I didn't tell them why.

———

Scene Four

No Placard. Enter a DOCTOR *and* DAVE.

DOCTOR   Ah, Mrs Taylor. Happy news. You're pregnant.

HELEN   I was shattered. So was Dave.

DAVE   What? But I thought you had that coil thing. I thought you were safe.

HELEN   Well, the hospital told me it was safe. First time he worries. First time he even thinks about it, is when it doesn't work. We were just starting to manage, too. Really getting on top of things with two wages coming in. Besides, I was glad to get out of the house to start meeting people again. Because I was happier, I got on better with the kids. I didn't know what to do. Dave wasn't much help. So I had a chat to Elsie next door and she said 'Look, love, you don't want to go back to years of washing nappies and scraping by to feed them all. You'll have to get rid of it.' She was right, but at the time it seemed all wrong to me, kind of — selfish, unnatural. Do you know what I mean?

DAVE   Well, I don't know what to do. I could do more overtime, I suppose. We might scrape by. But there's not much of that going about, these days, love. On the other hand, we could think of, sort of — not having it. But you do what you think's best for all of us, love. (*He exits*)

HELEN   So I made up my mind. I went to the doctor and I told him, straight. 'I don't want this child.'

DOCTOR   Now, Mrs Taylor, you must consider your responsibility to the unborn child.

HELEN   'Responsibilities for the unborn child? What about the two I've got already? What about me?' We argued about it for a bit.

DOCTOR   Mrs Taylor, I understand your feelings, but you must consider my position. Under the law as it now stands I can only terminate a pregnancy under the most stringent conditions. And in my opinion neither your physical nor your mental health is in danger, and as far as I can see, nor is there any grave risk to your family. However, I can put you in touch with a private clinic, provided, of course, that you get your husband's permission first. (*He exits*)

HELEN   It cost a lot of money, but we decided to go through with it and I had the abortion. I still wonder whether I did the right thing or not, but I knew I couldn't have faced being stuck at home again with another kid, shouting and screaming, like I used to at the others. I mean, how can you give a kiddie the love it needs if you don't feel right in yourself? If things had been different — if there were nurseries, if they'd give me time off work, then I might have had a real choice.

HELEN (*sings*)   Why is choosing and deciding always left to me
Have I learnt enough to really know what's best for me
So I can choose to be a mother when I want to be
Bearing children can be great — it's your natural estate,
It's a joy to watch them grow, it's what every woman knows
We can make the future theirs, give them all the love and care
But if I'm unhappy, what have I to give?
Can I teach them of the world when I'm not part of it?
Our children have inherited a world of life
Our duty is to build them a better life
Being a person not a mother is the start of it.
Women are not machines that do nothing but breed
Let them only bear the kids that they want, and need.
When I'm out at work I'm nearer to the heart of it.
When I clock on in the morning I've got friends there of my own
And it's not as someone's missus or a mum that I am known
We have a laugh and giggle and we talk of that and this
And I've learnt that life is more than just the current price of fish.
And when I take my wages home, though it isn't much, I grant
   you,

> We can pay our way for another day or buy the kids some new
>   shoes
> And though I lead a double life I know I've more to offer
> I'm a less dependent, understanding, tired wife and mother.
> Sure, life could be more easy and it isn't asking much,
> If they want us in their factories, give us nurseries and such,
> Give us more sex education, contraception and to spare
> Then we'll be free of choosing
> Between the risk of losing
> A seed as yet ungrown
> And a woman's life that has begun.

I've got a new job now, at the factory up the road. I'm getting on alright.

———————

Scene Five

Placard: 'The Disputed Pint'. An evening at the club. GEORGE, *a middle-aged shop steward at* HELEN'*s new workplace,* MARY, *his wife (!) and* MIKE, *a younger worker at the same workplace, are having a drink together.* MARY *has a 'short',* GEORGE *and* MIKE *are getting near the end of their 'pints'.*

MARY   Is that my drink, love?

GEORGE   Just a minute, love, just a minute. Now what you talking about, eh? (*To* MIKE) What do you mean?

MIKE   I'm just sick to death of it, that's all. It's been nothing but strike, strike, strike at that place.

GEORGE   Now look, we've had an overtime ban for five weeks, right. We've got them just where we want them . . . right? And what do you do? You turn round and say 'I've had enough!'

MIKE   It's alright for you, mate. I've got me motorbike to pay for.

MIKE continues mumbled complaints as HELEN *and* DAVE *enter.* MARY *sees them and points them out to* GEORGE. DAVE *brings on their drinks: a half for* HELEN *and a pint for himself. The glasses are half empty.*

GEORGE (*to* HELEN)   Hello, love. (*As part of a general greeting*)

HELEN   Dave, this is George, my shop steward. And this is Mike who works next to me. And . . . oh . . . I'm ever so sorry . . . I should have introduced Mary first.

MARY   Oh, don't worry, love. I'm used to it.

GEORGE (*embarrassed*) Oh . . . aye . . . the wife.

DAVE   Hello, love. (DAVE *and* HELEN *have now joined the others*)

HELEN (*to* MARY) Are you working?

MARY   Oh no. I've got my hands full with him and the kids. I don't know how you manage, honestly I don't.

> MARY *and* HELEN *continue talking to each other beneath the more voluble men's talk.*

MIKE (*to* GEORGE) Now look, I just can't afford to keep going out on strike.

GEORGE   I can't afford it. Nobody can afford it. But we've been going for parity for God knows how long and I'm telling you something, lad, if they don't come up with an offer by the end of the week, we're out. We'll shut that bloody factory down if we have to.

HELEN (*overhearing*) What's that, George? Shut the factory down?

GEORGE   That's right, love. Till they give us what we want.

HELEN (*to* MIKE) Does that mean our section too?

MIKE   I suppose it bloody well does.

GEORGE   Well, of course it does, doesn't it? I mean, you takes your choice. You either come out with us and make it a hundred per cent or you wait until they lay you off.

HELEN   Well, I wouldn't mind being consulted.

GEORGE   You should've been at the meeting, love.

HELEN   I couldn't, could I, George. It was in the evening. Dave wouldn't let me. You can ask him.

DAVE   Now come on, love. You can't have it both ways. I mean, someone's got to stay at home and look after the kids.

GEORGE   Oh . . . aye . . . it's a problem, that.

MIKE   Mmm . . . problem, that.

MARY   Typical!

HELEN   Now look. If you're all going out on strike and I'm going to be out of pocket, I wouldn't mind knowing why. What's this parity business all about? Does it mean everybody doing the same work?

DAVE   No, no, love, you don't know what you're talking about. What he's trying to say . . .

GEORGE   Hold on. Hold on, Dave. It's a fair question.

HELEN (*to* DAVE) See.

GEORGE   Look now. I'll show you. (*He stands*) Now I want you to imagine I'm Henry Ford, (*He takes up a boss's pose*)

MARY   I wish you were. (*Laughter*)

GEORGE   (*emphatic and impatient*) I'm Henry Ford. Now, I've got two factories, one in Coventry where Dave works, OK? And one here in — (*location of performance*) — where you — (HELEN) — and Mike work. Alright? Now, this is important, both factories are doing the same sort of work. Dave, could you do a bit of work, like?

DAVE   You what?

GEORGE   Pretend you're working.

MIKE   Go on, show us your stuff, Dave.

DAVE   You mean like this? (DAVE *mimes a work process with his hands*)

MIKE   (*to* HELEN) Is that what he spends all his time doing? (*Laughs*)

DAVE   Well, it's only pretend, isn't it?

GEORGE   (*irritated*) Come on now, are you listening?

WOMEN   Yes.

GEORGE   Now, I have to pay him wages at the end of the week, don't I? So I'm going to use this beer to pay him. Right?

DAVE   I like it.

GEORGE   End of the week. I pay him his wages.

DAVE *holds up his nearly empty glass.* GEORGE *fills it half full from a pipkin.* DAVE *drinks.*

GEORGE   Oh, don't drink it. I'm trying to show them something.

DAVE   Oh sorry. I thought . . .

MIKE   He's only here for the beer. (*Laughter.* GEORGE *is exasperated*)

GEORGE   Do it again. Dave, bring your glass back. Now, every week I pay him his wages. (*He half fills the glass again*) Now. What do you think of that?

DAVE   There's not much there, is there?

GEORGE   So what are you going to do about it?

DAVE   Eh?

GEORGE *signals to him to cotton on. It's for the benefit of the women.*

DAVE   Oh . . . yes . . . well, I want some more. Fill it up.

GEORGE   (*confidently, as Henry Ford*) I couldn't possibly afford to pay you more. The cost of raw materials, shrinking profit margins . . .

DAVE   Then I'm going on strike.

MIKE   He's got him over a barrel.

WOMEN   Eh?

MIKE   A barrel of beer. It's a joke.

GEORGE   Well, he's got a point. You see, no work from him, no profits for me. So I either have to pay up or in the end I'm going to have to cough up, aren't I?

MARY   And you won't do that, will you?

GEORGE   (*threatening*)   I'll do something in a minute.

GEORGE *fills* DAVE's *glass to the top.* MIKE *notices* DAVE *gets a drink and he doesn't.*

MIKE   Hey, what about me?

GEORGE   I'm coming to you. Now you're here in — (*location of performance*) — and you're doing the same work as Dave is in Coventry. So come on, lad, do a bit of work.

DAVE   Come on, clever dick, let's see you.

MIKE *mimes pulling a pint.*

GEORGE   It's supposed to be . . . oh never mind.

DAVE   (*to* MIKE)   Have to be different, don't you.

GEORGE   (*to* MIKE)   So at the end of the week I pay you your wages.

GEORGE *now fills* MIKE's *nearly empty pint half full from the pipkin.* MIKE *compares his half-full glass with* DAVE's *full one.*

MIKE   Hey, he's got more than me.

DAVE   Well, what are you going to do about it, lad?

MIKE   Oh bloody hell . . . go on strike.

GEORGE   That's it, lad. You go on strike for the same wages as Dave's getting. (*He fills up* MIKE's *glass*) It's only common sense, isn't it. Same wages for the same work. Now, Helen, that's what we call parity and that's what we're after.

DAVE   Cheers, Mike. (*They drink together*)

HELEN   Well, that's alright for you who can go on strike. But the more you take the less there is for everyone else. What about the hospital workers? What about old-age pensioners? They can't go on strike, can they? I don't think it's fair, I don't.

Uproar of disagreement.

DAVE   Alright. (*Quietening them*) Alright. Now, look, Nobody thinks that's fair. Nobody. But let's say, for the sake of argument, that I was to take less in my wages from my employer. That's what you're asking, isn't it? I should give some of it back. Come over here, Mr Ford. (*To* GEORGE) Give us your glass. (*He pours half his pint into* GEORGE*'s glass*) There. And I say: 'Please Mr Ford, will you kindly give that to the nurses and the old-age pensioners?' Well — does he?

GEORGE   Of course he doesn't. It's just more profit for Henry Ford. (*He drinks*) Cheers, Dave.

MIKE   Hey . . . , he's the bugger who ought to take a cut in wages. That Henry Ford.

GEORGE   That's what I've been trying to tell you. Takes bloody years, doesn't it?

HELEN   Well alright, maybe the hospital workers and old-age pensioners don't work for you, but I do. I work in the same place as Mike and what do I get out of it?

HELEN *holds up her nearly empty half pint against* MIKE*'s full pint.*

GEORGE   You obviously haven't understood, love. You see, when we get a rise, when we get to parity, you'll get more as well.

HELEN   Oh, will I?

GEORGE   Yes, love. You'll get the same as what the women are getting in Coventry. It's only fair.

GEORGE *fills up* HELEN*'s half pint from the pipkin.*

DAVE   It's only fair, that. Yes.

MIKE   Only fair.

HELEN *now holds up her full half pint against* MIKE*'s full pint.*

HELEN   I'm still not getting as much as Mike and I'm doing the same work.

GEORGE   Well, of course not, love. You're on a woman's rate.

DAVE   A woman's wage, love, you wouldn't get as much, would you? (MIKE *echoes agreement*)

HELEN   Oh . . . I see. I think I've got it. That means I should go on strike for parity with Mike. (*Uproar from the men*)

DAVE   No, no, love. You've got it all wrong. What you're talking about there is equal pay.

GEORGE   Equal pay.

DAVE   Not parity.

GEORGE/DAVE   That's completely different.

HELEN   Well, I don't see the difference. (*To the audience*) Do you? (*To* MARY) What do you think, Mary?

MARY   Well, I don't know . . .

GEORGE   Well, of course there's a difference . . .

MARY   Hang on . . .

GEORGE   Listen, there's . . .

MARY (*cutting him*)   Hang on. I don't know about this parity and equal pay thing, but what I do know is that I'm his cook, his nursemaid . . .

HELEN   His cleaner . . .

MARY   Yes, and his baby minder. And what do I get out of it?

GEORGE   My undying love and affection. (*The men laugh*)

DAVE   Who's for another beer then? (*The men are*)

HELEN   George. (*She lifts up a pint glass*) I think I'll have a pint this time.

MEN (*to each other*)   Hello!

———

Scene Six. Placard: 'Never Keep a Lady Waiting'.

An electronic components factory. The red ladder is set back stage. A management figure JOHNSON *enters with an umbrella. He climbs the ladder and has the following conversation with the managing* DIRECTOR *who is heard from offstage.*

DIRECTOR   Hello? Johnson?

JOHNSON   Oh hello. Yes, sir?

DIRECTOR   Look, they've been on strike for over five weeks now.

JOHNSON   Yes. I know, sir.

DIRECTOR   Well, I want this parity thing settled immediately.

JOHNSON   Yes, sir. Righty ho, sir. And what about the women's demand for equal pay?

DIRECTOR   On no account give way to that. It will set a precedent for the whole corporation and cost us a fortune.

JOHNSON   Yes. I see.

DIRECTOR   No equal pay, understand. If the worst comes to the worst we'll offer them a job evaluation and try and get round it that way.

JOHNSON   Fine. I'll try that.

JOHNSON *opens his umbrella. Holding it face on to the audience he disappears behind it. Letters read PROFIT round the umbrella top. Enter* GEORGE, *the shop steward, and* JOHN, *a trade union negotiator. They meet on stage.*

JOHN   George!

GEORGE   Hello, John. Where have you been?

JOHN   Sorry I'm late, George. I got held up in these bloody negotiations at GEC. Took two hours. Now, how are things going here?

GEORGE   Oh fine. Fine. The lads are going to pull it through. Don't you worry.

JOHN   Good. Good. And what about the women?

GEORGE   Oh, it's the same old story. You never see them down the picket line. They're probably all at home knitting.

JOHN   Now come on, George. You know what I'm talking about. What about this equal pay claim?

GEORGE   Well, you know how I stand on that. If we could just have some adjustment —

JOHN   Now seriously, George, head office are dead keen on recruiting women and they're red hot on this one.

GEORGE   Well, head office doesn't have to work on the shop floor, do they? Alright. Equal pay, so long as we get parity first. Some of the men are going to go barmy.

JOHN   Don't worry now. We're strong enough to win the both of them.

JOHNSON *appears from behind the umbrella.*

JOHNSON   Gentlemen? If you're ready?

JOHN   Right then.

GEORGE *and* JOHN *go to the ladder. Each climbs half way up a different side. They are now a pyramid of three with* JOHNSON *at the top, still holding the umbrella open, top out to the audience.* JOHNSON *shakes* JOHN's *hand.*

JOHNSON   Hello there, John, nice to see you again. (*He turns to* GEORGE *and offers his hand.* GEORGE *doesn't take it*) Hello.

GEORGE   How do. (*Mouths 'bastard'*)

JOHNSON   I see. Right.

All three then swoop in behind the umbrella. An aggressive, improvised negotiation argument takes place for a few seconds. Hands, fists, and fingers gesticulate from behind the umbrella. The babble suddenly stops. All heads pop out.

JOHNSON   I have no mandate from my board to settle this claim.

JOHN   Don't you give me that line.

GEORGE   Bloody rubbish. I'm off.

JOHNSON   However . . . (GEORGE, *about to leave, stays at the prospect of concession from* JOHNSON) . . . what about parity . . . but in stages?

JOHN   Stages?

GEORGE (*aggressively*)   Stages!

JOHNSON   Yes . . . how about the end of 1978?

GEORGE   We want it now!

JOHNSON   '76?

JOHN   Late 1975.

JOHNSON   Agreed.

GEORGE (*to the audience*)   Good day's work there. Get off home now. (*He makes to leave*)

JOHN   What about the women's demand for equal pay, George?

GEORGE (*caught out*)   Oh . . . aye . . . equal pay. (*He returns to the ladder*)

All three in behind the ladder again but this time the aggression is gone. The argument is sweeter. JOHNSON *appears.*

JOHNSON   No. No, I'm afraid until reorganisation the ladies will just have to wait. (*He returns behind the umbrella*)

Sweeter argument now gives way to the telling of sexist jokes behind the umbrella.

GEORGE   Here . . . have you heard the one about — (*Babble and laughter*) . . . and he said: 'What do you think these are, pickled onions?' (*Laughter*) Then she said: 'Never keep a lady waiting!'

All three come out from behind the umbrella roaring with laughter. They stop, mutually embarrassed. Then dive behind again. The argument resumes its aggression. They appear again.

JOHNSON   If that's the attitude you're going to take about equal pay, you can forget all about your parity claim.

Now JOHN *makes to leave.*

GEORGE   Steady on, John.

JOHNSON   What about a job evaluation scheme?

GEORGE   Eh?

JOHN (*returning*)   Not without union control.

JOHNSON   Very well.

GEORGE/JOHN   We've won.

JOHNSON (*to the audience*)   I've won. (GEORGE *and* JOHN *exit.* JOHNSON *stays on the ladder behind the umbrella*)

Enter HELEN *and* SHEILA, *another worker in the factory. They sit down at their work bench. The work, when it takes place, is the mimed soldering of components to printed circuits.*

SHEILA   Well, she told me she waited until she were married.

HELEN   Oh yes? Did you?

SHEILA   Did I heck!

Enter CHRISSIE, *aged about seventeen.* HELEN *and* SHEILA *are working.*

HELEN   When are you getting married, Chrissie?

CHRISSIE   Oh, I've had second thoughts.

SHEILA   Oh dear. What's the matter this time?

CHRISSIE   Well, he drinks a lot, you know.

HELEN   Oh does he?

CHRISSIE   And they're not much good at it when they've been drinking, now, are they?

SHEILA   No they're not. My husband were like that.

CHRISSIE   Oh yes? What did you do?

SHEILA   I told him: if you come home drunk again you're not having it.

CHRISSIE   Did it work?

SHEILA   Oh, it worked alright. I've not seen him for five years.

CHRISSIE   Well I won't try that then, will I?

HELEN   I might.

CHRISSIE   What I really wanted to know was . . . what's it like after five years with the same bloke night after night?

HELEN   Well, it's not night after night after five years, love. You get used to it.

SHEILA   You get bloody fed up with it.

Enter MIKE.

CHRISSIE   Oooh. . . here he comes . . . Alvin Stardust back on the line. Hey Alvin, how do you get your hair to go like that?

MIKE   Get knotted. (*He sits with them on the line and starts working*)

HELEN   Oh, Chrissie. I like his action, don't you?

CHRISSIE (*sings*)   Something in the way he walks . . . .

WOMEN   Reminds me of no other lover . . . .

MIKE   You're just jealous. (*To the audience*) Makes you bloody sick.

Enter the TIME AND MOTION MAN, *or Job Evaluator. He wears a white coat and has glasses on with clock faces for the lenses. He carries a clipboard and pencil.*

T & M (*to the audience*)   Trouble with the workforce? Need a solution? Speed up, rationalisation, measured day work . . . you name it, I evaluate it. Now — today's little problem. (*Pointing to the workers*) This lot here. The women are going for equal pay, but to get that they have to prove that the work they're doing is the same or of a broadly similar nature to what the men are doing.

JOHNSON (*appearing from behind the ladder*)   And we have to prove that it isn't. (*He disappears again*)

T & M   And that's where I come in. Now . . . let's see what the women are actually doing, shall we? (*He looks them over*) Oh yes. Well, they're only fitting up components. Now — let's have a look at the man. (*Looks*) Oh dear. He's fitting up components. This is going to be tricky. Still, press on, eh? (*To the women*) Good morning, ladies.

CHRISSIE   Hello.

SHEILA   Hello. Trouble!

T & M   Right (*He examines* CHRISSIE'*s work*) Number one. (*Consulting his clipboard*) Skill. (*To* CHRISSIE) Well, that doesn't look too difficult to me, dear.

CHRISSIE   Oh no. It's not really.

HELEN   It's very fiddly . . . detailed. You have to be quick with your hands.

SHEILA   Yes. A bloke couldn't do this job. They're too clumsy.

CHRISSIE   But it's ever so boring.

JOHNSON (*popping out*)   Actually, we do find that our female operatives are naturally suited to boring monotonous work. (*Pops back*)

T & M   Boring. I'll put that down for the women then. (*Makes a note*) Right. Now let's have a look at the man. (*To* MIKE) Oh . . . that does look extremely difficult to me, sir, if you don't mind my saying so.

MIKE   Piss off, will you, pal. I'm busy.

T & M (*to the audience*)   Did you see that? No time to natter, this lad. Far too busy. Not like the girls, eh? (*Writes*) High degree of concentration required. (*To* MIKE) It does look extremely difficult and complicated, sir.

MIKE   Well, of course it's complicated. It's all complicated, isn't it, girls?

WOMEN   Yes.

T & M (*to the audience*)   Oh well. Win a few, lose a few. (*Writes*) Same degree of skill required on the basic operation.

MIKE *moves from the line, bends down and picks something up.* T & M *perks up.*

T & M   How many times a day do you do that?

MIKE   Get stuffed.

T & M (*to the audience*)   Did you see that? Turn, lift, load . . . that's physical effort, that is. And what if he dropped it? (*Writes*) High degree of responsibility required. Now . . . that's two point three times five point nine add the weighting factor and take away the number you first thought of . . . now. — Let's see . . . oh yes . . . surprise surprise . . . men — pay scale three . . . women scale four.

SHEILA   How do you get that then?

T & M   Well, it's all in the figures, dear. Extremely complicated. You wouldn't understand.

SHEILA   What do you mean? In the figures?

T & M   Well, it's all sorts of things like skill, initiative, training.

HELEN   We never get a chance to be trained.

SHEILA   That's right. I applied but they wouldn't give it to a woman.

T & M   Well . . . that's nothing to do with me. I'm just the job evaluator. (*To the audience*) It's all scientific. (*He moves to go but the women grab hold of him*)

SHEILA   Scientific? You won't get away with that.

HELEN   No. We're doing the same work as the men.

T & M   But look — physical effort.

SHEILA   Physical effort? What about our backs?

HELEN   Yes — I get a crick in mine bending over all day.

SHEILA   And I'm going boss-eyed staring at all them little circuits.

HELEN   We're not standing for this.

SHEILA   No, we're not.

They have now forced T & M *upstage. As they are about to go for him* JOHNSON *brings his umbrella neatly down over to protect* T & M.

JOHNSON (*to the* DIRECTOR *on the phone*) Hello, sir.

DIRECTOR (*from offstage*) Yes. What is it?

JOHNSON The job evaluator's managed to put the women one grade below the men but I'm afraid they're kicking up a bit of a stink about it.

DIRECTOR Well, tell them if they're not careful, we'll close the whole place down.

JOHNSON Try that old chestnut on them, eh, sir? Righty - ho.

Scene Seven

Placard: 'Parity begins at home'. HELEN *and* DAVE'*s bedroom.* HELEN *comes in and starts making the bed.*

VOICE OFF Mum.

HELEN Oh, what is it, Peter? Are you still up, love?

PETER I can't sleep, Mum.

HELEN Oh, alright, I'll be with you in a minute (*She goes off*)

Enter DAVE, *dressed only in towel and socks, humming 'Something in the way I move'. He admires his body in the mirror, takes off towel, to reveal his natty underpants, jumps into bed.*

DAVE Helen.

HELEN (*from downstairs*) Yes, what is it?

DAVE You coming, love?

HELEN Ay, in a minute. I'm just finishing your shirt.

DAVE Oh. (DAVE *looks around guiltily, picks out* Playboy *magazine from under the bed and begins to look at the dirty pictures. Stripper music fades up on tape.* DAVE *becomes involved in it, begins humming tune. Stripper music fades down on tape,* HELEN *comes on stage.* DAVE *is caught in the act of getting into the pictures*) Oh, there you are, love, I was just waiting for you. (HELEN *gets into bed*) There, snug as a bug in a rug, eh?

HELEN (*kisses* DAVE) Goodnight, love. (*She lies down*)

DAVE (*left stranded, he then snuggles up to her*) Here, you've washed your hair — smells really nice.

HELEN (*turns over*) Ooh, I am tired.

DAVE (*looks at audience in desperation, tries again*) Come on, Helen, love.

HELEN It's late. I've got to get up at half past six.

DAVE (*sits up, exasperated*) I don't know what's happening to us, I really don't.

HELEN I'm sorry, I'm tired.

DAVE You're always too tired these days. You call this a marriage?

HELEN So it's my fault, is it? What were you doing this evening?

DAVE Watching tele.

HELEN And what was I doing?

DAVE Watching tele.

HELEN Yes, and doing the ironing. And last night it was the washing. I come home from work and I have to start all over again and you wonder why I'm tired.

DAVE I did warn you before you started work that it might be too much for you. Bloody good thing if you do get the push from this job of yours, if you ask me. At least things'd start getting back to normal round here.

HELEN You're beginning to sound like my boss. When it suits him I've got to give up my job, when it suits you I've got to give up my job. Well, did it ever occur to you that I don't want to give up my job?

DAVE Well, if that's what you want, why don't you stop complaining and let me get some sleep, will you.

HELEN I'm not complaining about having a job, I'm complaining about having two — one in the factory and one here.

DAVE What do you mean? Two jobs? When you married me, you said that was all you ever wanted out of life, and now you've got it, you do nothing but moan. You're never satisfied, woman.

HELEN They're your kids too, you know. And it was your shirt this evening I was ironing. What do you think I am, a bloody laundry service? Why can't you iron your own shirts.

DAVE Because that's what I married you for. If I'd have thought things were going to turn out like this, I would have stayed single and had some fun. At least I wouldn't have a wife and two kids hanging round my neck.

HELEN So that's all we are to you, is it?

DAVE Well, don't blame me for feeling like that. You're the one that's ruining everything, not me. Don't you love me and the kids? Eh?

HELEN But what about me? Do you love me?

DAVE   Well, yes, of course I do, love. That's why I'm saying, you should give up your job because it's obviously too much for you, isn't it?

HELEN   No, Dave, I'm not giving up my job. I'm not going back to asking you every time I want a bob or two for something. Oh, look, Dave. Work's not that marvellous, but for the first time I've got a life of my own outside these four walls. I've got friends of my own at work. And with this closure threat, we've got a real fight on our hands. So, you're just going to have to start helping at home. You can start — with the ironing.

DAVE   Oh, no. You're not getting me doing woman's work.

HELEN   You'll soon do it, love — if no one does it for you. (*They exit*)

Placard: 'The Maintenance Engineer'. A woman, not HELEN, *sings —*

SONG   One Friday night it happened
some years after we were wed
when my old man come home from work
as usual, I said:
'Your tea is on the table
your clothes are on the rack
your bath'll soon be ready.
I'll come up and scrub your back.'
He kissed me very tenderly
and said 'I'll tell you, flat,
the service I give my machine
ain't half as good as that'.

I said: 'I'm not your little woman
your sweetheart or your dear,
I'm a wage slave without wages,
I'm a maintenance engineer.'
And then we got to talking
I told him how I felt
how I kept him running just as smooth
as some conveyor belt.
For after all, it's I'm the one
provides the power supply
he goes just like the clappers
on my steak and kidney pie.
His fittings are all shiny
'cos I keep them nice and clean
and I told him his machine tool
is the best I've ever seen —

but

I'm not (etc) . . .

The terms of my employment
would make your hair turn grey
I have to be on call, you see,
for twenty-four hours a day.
I quite enjoy the perks, though,
when I'm working through the night
we get job satisfaction
well, *he* will and p'raps I might.
If I keep up full production
with another kid or two
some future boss will have a brand-new
labour force to screw . . .

but

I'm not (etc) . . .

The truth began to dawn then
how I keep him fit and trim
so the boss can make a nice fat profit
out of me and him.
And as a solid union man
he got in quite a rage
to think that we're both working hard
and getting one man's wage.
I said 'And what about the part-time
packing job I do?
That's three men that I work for, love,
my boss, your boss and you.'
I said:

I'm not (etc) . . .

He looked a litle sheepish
and said 'As from today,
The lads and me'll see what we
can do on equal pay.
Would you like a housewives' union,
do you think you should be paid
as a cook, and as a cleaner,
as a nurse and as a maid?'
I said 'Don't jump the gun, love,
if you did your share at home,

then I might have some time to fight
some battles of my own.'

I'm not (etc) . . .

━━━━━━

Scene Eight

Placard: 'The way to a man's heart is through his stomach'. The factory,
SHEILA, LEN, CHRISSIE *and* MIKE *are working.*

SHEILA   Did you fix it up at the canteen, then?

HELEN   Ay, I did.

SHEILA   Are they coming out with us?

HELEN   They are.

SHEILA   Eh, this is going to be a laugh. I can hardly wait.

HELEN   You won't have to. It's twelve o'clock.

SHEILA   Twelve o'clock, girls. You know what that means.

SHEILA *and* HELEN *stop working.*

HELEN (*to* CHRISSIE)   Come on, Chrissie, love. It's twelve o'clock.

MIKE   Hey, what's going on? It's not dinner time yet.

HELEN   Well, I think they call it a 'down tools'.

MIKE   But you can't do that. You'll stop the whole process.

SHEILA   That's the general idea.

MIKE   Well, have you talked to the shop steward yet?

SHEILA *and* HELEN   No.

MIKE   You women don't know nothing, do you?

SHEILA *and* HELEN   No.

MIKE   I better go and do it, then. (*He exits*)

HELEN   Come on, Chrissie, love, it's twelve o'clock.

CHRISSIE   Here, I don't like this.

SHEILA   Look, love, if you want equal pay, you'll have to put up a fight for it.
    They'll never —

CHRISSIE   Yes, that's just the point. I don't think I do want equal pay. I mean,
    my boy friend, he says it makes a man feel inferior and I agree with him.

HELEN   Well, if that's his attitude, love, then he is inferior.

SHEILA   My husband were like that. The one thing that gave him a bit of comfort was knowing there was someone worse off than him — me.

Enter GEORGE *and* MIKE.

GEORGE   Now then, girls, what's all this commotion here? What's going on?

HELEN   It's this job evaluation, George. They downgraded us and we're not standing for it.

GEORGE   Look, how many times must I . . . the shop stewards committee is already considering your case.

HELEN   And how much longer are they going to consider it? When are you going to do something?

GEORGE   They've got a lot on their plate, you know. Now listen, you can't just do what you want, you must stick to procedure on this.

SHEILA   We did, George. We even brought it up at a branch meeting and what happened, eh?

HELEN   Show him, Sheila.

GEORGE   Look, I haven't got time to mess —

SHEILA   Alright, I will. (*She stands up and takes off a male shop steward addressing a meeting*) 'Right, brothers. Any other business? Oh, I do believe a sister here wants to say something.' (*She turns to* GEORGE) 'Come on, dear, don't be shy.' (*The other women whistle and make kissing noises*) 'Well, that's very interesting and we'll forward that to the District Committee and I'm sure they'll give it their fullest consideration. Right, now, if there's no other business, I'll close the meeting and there's just time for a quick one before they shut.'

GEORGE   Have you finished?

SHEILA   I have.

GEORGE   Now listen, don't you try and make a monkey out of me.

HELEN   That's why we want a mass meeting, George.

GEORGE   A mass meeting?

SHEILA   A mass meeting.

GEORGE   Oh, come on, girls, it's nearly dinner time. Why don't we all pop down to the canteen, have a nice bite to eat and a cup of tea and talk it over amongst ourselves.

HELEN   Oh, no, George. We women can't afford to eat in the canteen on our wages.

SHEILA   Besides, we feel uncomfortable with all you skilled men.

GEORGE   Uuugh — women. (*Bumps into* MIKE) Get out of my bloody way, will you.

Exit MIKE *and* GEORGE. HELEN *and* SHEILA *laugh.*

SHEILA   That got him rattled.

HELEN   Yes, I hope he's hungry.

SHEILA   Hey up, what's up with our Chrissie.

HELEN   Chrissie, are you going to come out with us or not?

CHRISSIE   Oh, I'll have to ask me boy friend.

HELEN   Look, love, when I first got married I used to let my husband make all the decisions. After a while you begin to feel like half a person. You've got to start making up your own mind.

Enter GEORGE

GEORGE   Alright, now this has gone far enough.

MIKE *enters, bearing placard which he shows to the audience. Placard: 'If you want a square meal, give us a square deal — equal pay'.*

MIKE   Look at this. Now the bloody canteen women have come out on strike. (*To the women*) This is all your doing, isn't it.

WOMEN   Yes.

GEORGE   Now just a minute, lad —

MIKE   This lot are never satisfied. You don't do the overtime, you don't do the night shift. (*To the audience*) Well, what right have they got to equal pay, eh?

CHRISSIE   Yes, that's what my boy friend says. (*To* HELEN) Here, I don't want to work the night shift if I get equal pay.

SHEILA   No, love, the point is that no one should have to work the night shift or do all that overtime.

MIKE   Oh, bloody hell. I'm going for some fish and chips. (*To the audience*) I hate fish and chips. (*He exits*)

HELEN   Now look, George, you told me that trade unions are for getting better conditions, not worse. Well, we women have got better conditions. We don't do the night shift. So you men shouldn't be trying to drag us down to your level. Maybe you men should go on strike for parity conditions with us. We'd support you.

GEORGE   Eh? Oh come on, girls, look, you know I'm behind you, but I hope you realise that management have threatened to close this place down because of you.

SHEILA   Oh, George, if we fell for that one every time, none of us would get anywhere, would we?

GEORGE   You're asking the lads to put their jobs in jeopardy for you.

HELEN   That's why we want a mass meeting to put our case to the men.

SHEILA   And if we don't get one, we're still going out.

HELEN   So you can take your choice: either come out with us and make it a hundred per cent, or wait until they lay you off.

GEORGE   Alright, girls, I'll set it up. One of you can talk to the men, alright?

HELEN   You do that, Sheila.

SHEILA   Oh no, not me. I'd lose me temper. You do it, love.

CHRISSIE   Yes, you do it.

> CHRISSIE *and* SHEILA *exit.*

GEORGE   (*turns round, addresses the audience as though they were a works meeting*)   Alright, now, bit of hush at the back, now come on, settle down. Now, we've got little Helen along here to talk to you on behalf of the women, so I want you to put your hands together and show your usual sign of appreciation. (*Encourages the audience to applaud* HELEN) Alright, love. Nice big voice.

HELEN   Well, I expect you're probably wondering what all the fuss is about. I mean, equal pay is the law in 1975, so why don't we wait till the end of the year. But the fact is that job evaluation has put the women in our section one grade below the men so we won't get equal pay — not this year, next year, never. So we've got to take action now if we're ever going to get anywhere and we're asking you to support us in this fight.

> *Applause.* GEORGE *conducts the meeting, asks for questions from the floor.*

WORKER   (*from the audience*)   I see your point, love, but what you girls don't seem to realise is, the reason a man gets more than a woman is because he's got a family to support. Am I right? I mean, he's not in it for a bit of pin money, bit of extra. No, I'm sorry. I don't believe in equal pay. No.

FRED   (*an old worker*)   George, George, over here, George.

GEORGE   (*sees him*)   Alright, come on, Fred.

FRED   You think you're so flaming militant, don't you, the lot of you. The number of times I've heard blokes in this factory say, and you're one of them, George, 'If only the bloody women'd get involved and show a bit of fight.' Well, here they are, lads. They're ready to walk out them gates and we should support them.

Applause and cheers from women.

MIKE (*waving his arms from the back*) It's a flaming hunger strike, that's what it is. It's a flaming hunger strike. They're on strike and we go hungry. When are they going to open the canteen? That's what I want to know.

CANTEEN WOMAN We'll agree to open the canteen when you agree to support our strike. Until then, we're only going to feed the women. So think on it, brother.

ANOTHER WORKER George. Through the chair, George. Now look, normally I would support the women's demand for equal pay, I really would. But. We got to face facts. The management's threatened to close the whole place down and if it comes to a choice, between equal pay and the jobs of family men like you and me, well, I've just got to say no. I mean, lovely speech, dear, but no, I'm sorry.

SHEILA George. George. Well, I've got three kids and I haven't got a husband supporting me. I have to bring my kids up on the miserable pittance I earn here and I want a living wage like you.

Pandemonium, with GEORGE *trying to keep order.*

WORKER You're a bloody exception, dear. She's not what we're talking about.

SHEILA An exception? Are all the single men here exceptions, then? They don't have families to support. Perhaps you think they should take a cut in wages, do you? Honestly, some of you men are as thick as two short planks.

Pandemonium. GEORGE *trying to keep order.*

MIKE Open the bloody canteen.

GEORGE Will you shut up about the canteen. Now, I'm going to let Helen have the last word, so a bit of hush, please.

HELEN Well, first of all, none of us is working for pin money. We're all working for essentials. But it's more than that. We women don't always want to depend on our husbands. If you're lucky, you get a good husband and he gives you the money, and if you're unlucky you do without and you might get a black eye for your trouble. Either way, you ask, and he decides. Well, we want the right to work too. For a living wage just like you men, and that means equal pay for a start.

MAN Yes, but what about our jobs, love?

HELEN Do you think I want to lose my job? Can't you see? It's a management trick to keep our wages down and their bloody profits up and they're trying it on us women because they think we're weak, because they think you won't support us. Well, mark my words, if you don't support us, next time it'll be you electricians, then it'll be you draughtsmen, then it'll be you fitters. What we're saying is, we've all got to support each other. Then we'll win this fight just like we all won parity.

Applause.

GEORGE   Thank you, Helen, thank you. I'm going to put my two penn'orth in for what it's worth now.

MIKE   Open the canteen!

GEORGE (*to* MIKE) Just once more, do you hear, just once more. (*To the meeting*) I think we really should support these women in their fight.

MAN   Bloody rubbish, George.

Pandemonium.

GEORGE   Hang on, hang on. I know it's difficult, I know it's not easy. But after all you must agree that their fight is our fight. And besides, you heard what they said. (*To* MIKE) And you heard what she said. You want some dinner? Get your bloody hand up. (*To the meeting*) Right. All those in favour.

HELEN *holds up placard with question mark on it.*

———————

Scene Nine

Placard: 'Strike while the iron is hot'.

DAVE *and* HELEN*'s kitchen.* DAVE *is ironing. He burns his hand on the iron.*

DAVE   Ow. (*To the audience*) Alright, alright, wipe that smile off your face. I mean, you've got to help out sometimes, haven't you? It's only fair to the wife. And for those of you among us who've never done this before — it may look easy. But you know, I've found out it involves a fair amount of skill. It's boring, but it involves a fair amount of skill. Any old idiot can do a pillow case but to be able to do a shirt — oh, completely different.

Enter HELEN.

HELEN   Dave, you'll never guess what's happened, love.

DAVE (*surprised*) Oh, I've got a hot iron here, love.

HELEN   Oh, I'm sorry. I'll do it for you, shall I?

DAVE   No, it's alright, I'm on the last one.

HELEN   Oh. Well, shall I put the tea on, then?

DAVE   Tea's on. Kids have had their grub. Everything's under control.

HELEN   Is there nothing I can do?

DAVE   Yes, why don't you just sit down and tell me what's happened, eh?

HELEN   Well, we got the shop stewards to call a mass meeting.

DAVE   Mass meeting, eh?

HELEN   And the girls chose me to make a speech.

DAVE   You?

HELEN   Yes. I was dead nervous but then some of the men started yelling things and I got so angry I forgot all about being scared.

DAVE   And?

HELEN   They took a vote.

DAVE   Yes?

HELEN   They agreed to support us. We're coming out on strike tomorrow.

DAVE   Oh, that's really good, love. Might mean a bit more money coming in. We could do with that. (DAVE *picks up a sheet*) Give us a hand with this, will you, love? (*This sequence involves the folding of a sheet*)

DAVE   I can remember the time when you used to argue with me about even being in the union. (*To the audience*) Not bad, eh?

HELEN   There's another mass meeting on Saturday.

DAVE   Oh yes? You going, are you?

HELEN   I'm chairing it.

DAVE   Oh. Who's going to look after the kids then?

HELEN   Well, we've organised a play group so that more of the women can get involved.

DAVE   Oh, that's a really good idea. Yes. You go to your meeting and I can go to the football Saturday. Yes.

HELEN   Well, actually, love . . .

DAVE   Yes?

HELEN   I put you down for the playgroup.

The sheet is now folded. DAVE *is holding it. He drops it in amazement.*

DAVE   You did what?

HELEN   Well, I didn't know you had a football match.

DAVE   Well, you can bloody well take me off again because I'm going to the football Saturday.

HELEN   Oh now look, Dave, I stayed home all last weekend so you could go to your union weekend school.

DAVE   Oh, trust you to bring that up. Now look, Helen, I don't mind looking after my own two, but I do draw the line at other people's kids. Why can't the other husbands look after them?

HELEN   Well, some of the women haven't got husbands, and some of the husbands work on Saturdays, and besides, love, not all of them are as good with kids as you are.

DAVE   Yes, that's true. Oh, no, you're not going to get round me that way. That won't work.

HELEN   Well, Emily's husband's going to do it.

DAVE   What, old Fred? (*Laughs. To the audience*) You don't know old Fred. Now that would be worth seeing. Fred with nappies.

HELEN   So you don't mind, love?

DAVE   No, I'm not going. No.

HELEN   Well, I'll just go next door and see Elsie before tea then.

DAVE   Yes, you do that.

HELEN   It's important, Dave. If we start out weak, we'll never win. (*She exits*)

DAVE   You think I don't know it's important? I taught you everything you know about trade unionism. Bloody hell. (*He exits*)

Two banners are placed in front of the audience, one saying 'Workers will never be free while women are in chains' and the other 'Women will never be free while workers are in chains'.

CAST   Workers fight in many lands
and freedom is their aim
but the fight can only be half won
while women are in chains.
We got to stand together
if we can
stand together
every woman, every man.

The fascists marched on Cable Street
'They shall not pass,' we cried
we built the East End barricades
with dockers at our side
in the Easter of '16
we fought for Ireland's freedom
at the side of Connolly

we fought in Saigon province
at the side of Ho Chi Minh
brought down a Yankee bomber
in the hills of Do I Bin.
We got to stand together
and we can
stand together
every woman, every man.

So call us sweetheart if you like
but don't say that we're meek
we're workers just the same as you,
without us you are weak
we service men and children
and we're stuck at home all day
work part-time in the sweatshops
get the factories' lowest pay
the bosses live off all our backs
divide us with their lies
men and women, white and black,
let's fight, let's organise.
We got to stand together
you know we can
stand together
every woman, every man.

So sisters, brothers, organise
remember first and last
that power to the sisters must mean
power to the class.
We got to stand together
we can
every woman, every man.

Enter HELEN.

HELEN (*to the audience*) You don't count as a woman without a husband so you get married. But you're not much of a wife without kids so you stay at home. But you can't be a good mother without money so you go out to work. But you can't be a good worker and a good mother so you stay, underpaid, untrained and you do a second shift at home. But you're not a good wife when you're tired so you don't count as a woman.

We fight against all these things and what we've achieved is a beginning. But the fight won't end while we keep asking for crumbs. We've got to fight for something different. A world where children can grow up under decent conditions, where women can choose when to have kids, where we have free contraception and, when we need it, abortion. Where women can choose not to have kids and that's just as natural as having them. A world where women really are men's equals, not just with equal pay — that's just equal exploitation — but a world with no exploitation. This means big changes and only you and I can make them. But if they're needed, can you say we're asking too much?

THE END

CARE AND CONTROL
Gay Sweatshop

During 1976 Gay Sweatshop was touring with its first women's show, *Any Woman Can,* by Jill Posener. We used to have discussions after the play, and ask people in the audiences what sort of play they would like to see us do next. A number of people suggested that we should do a play which drew attention to the problems facing lesbian mothers in custody cases— there had been cases in which children had been taken away from their mothers because the court considered that the mother's lesbianism was harmful to the child.

Two lesbian mothers said they were willing to talk about their experiences, and we started compiling a dossier of primary and secondary source material. Nancy did most of the research in early 1977, interviewing mothers, lawyers, children, speaking to the Association for Lesbian Parents, the Rights of Women (a group of feminist lawyers) and an organisation for one-parent families. We taped interviews to use as the basis for the play, and to help the cast with material for improvisations.

The company drew up a rough scenario, based on our research, and over five weeks did a detailed synopsis, using improvisations which some members of the company then wrote up. During this time Mary Moore was taking slides of day-to-day life with the children, and Terri Quaye was writing the music. We arrived at a point where we had a lot of material, but felt we could not produce an adequate script ourselves. We asked Michelene Wandor (with whom we had briefly discussed the project the year before) to come in and script it. This involved taking our characters, scenario and story, writing original material where necessary, editing and tightening and reorganising material we already had. This was done in discussion with the company, and the play opened in London, at the Drill Hall, in May 1977. A week before, we gave an informal reading/rehearsal to an audience which included many of the women who had helped us with our research — it was emotionally affecting as these women recognised aspects of their experiences, and felt some gratification that we had accurately represented some of the dilemmas in which mothers find themselves. This sense of recognition from audiences was a consistent part of the response during the time we performed the play.

Our publicity leaflet contained the following:

'*Care and Control* is based on the experiences of lesbian mothers in their fight for custody of their children. The situations in the play are taken from life and have been adapted to preserve the anonymity of women who are still struggling in the court.

Single mothers, lesbian and heterosexual, face the same kind of prejudice when they come before the judicial system. A woman is suspect in the eyes of the State when she asserts her right to live independently of men. She is seen as a direct challenge to family life and the traditional sexual roles which the courts uphold.

It is against these attitudes and assumptions, which deny all of us the right to decide the most basic and intimate matters of our lives, that women are organising to fight the custody battle. It is a dramatic development — one which the women of Gay Sweatshop wished to explore, not only for the sake of representing the struggle, but also to advance it.'

In basing the play on real-life events we were consciously relating our work to actual political struggle, as well as trying to produce good theatre. We developed three parallel stories in Act One to show how women in very different situations face the same prejudices, and how they cope in their day-to-day lives. The style of this Act is naturalistic and informal. In Act Two we wanted to show how the impersonal court process is alienated from the lives of ordinary people, and therefore created a legal and formal atmosphere in which two of the court cases were intercut and seen in greater detail, and through which we could demonstrate the arguments more clearly to the audiences.

The play toured with its original cast throughout spring and summer of 1977, and was then recast for the Edinburgh Festival in September 1977, and further touring. It was performed by the Rose Bruford College of Speech and Drama in the autumn of 1978.

The play was very well received everywhere, and was enthusiastically reviewed — people grasped the arguments and appreciated the theatricality of the piece.

Kate Crutchley
Nancy Diuguid

Care and Control was first performed in May 1977 at the Drill Hall, 16 Chenies St., London WC1.

CAST

SARA	Kate Phelps
STEPHEN	Michael Kellan
CAROL	Natasha Fairbanks
SUE	Helen Barnaby
CHRIS	Kate Crutchley
ELIZABETH	Nancy Diuguid
GERALD	Michael Kellan

RECAST FOR AUTUMN 1977

SARA	Libby Mason
STEPHEN	Martin Panter
CAROL	Sara Hardy
SUE	Marilyn Milgrom
CHRIS	Jill Posener
ELIZABETH	Patricia Donovan
GERALD	Martin Panter

Researched by Nancy Diuguid
Devised by the original company and Priscilla Allen
Scripted by Michelene Wandor
Music by Terri Quaye
Designed by Mary Moore
Directed by Kate Crutchley

ACT ONE

Scene One

The set is very simple. Straw matting defines the playing area, and at the back is a large screen or a blank wall on which to project slides. The colour of the matting and screen should blend if possible. There is a table and two chairs up-centre, just in front of the screen. Downstage right is a heap of cushions on the floor, and downstage left two low wooden boxes with padded tops, each about three feet square, are placed end to end to represent bed/bench as required. If music is used the musicians can be placed in the background, wherever it is most convenient.

> *Pulse music: 'Inception'. The cast enter and sit or stand.* CAROL *sits on the heap of cushions,* SUE *on the boxes.* CHRIS *operates slides of a pregnant woman in hospital over the dialogue.*

AUTHORITY (CHRIS) Normal labour begins in one of three ways. One: the onset of contractions — what used to be called labour pains. Two: the breaking of the waters. This is the rupturing of the sac of amniotic fluid in which baby has spent his nine months. Three: a show. The little plug of mucus which seals the neck of the womb comes away. Any of these may be accompanied by backache or discomfort similar to period pains.

SARA When I told my GP I wanted to have it, she nearly had a fit. 'Why?' she said. 'It's quite normal,' I said. 'Some women want babies and some women don't want babies. I want a baby.'
'But a baby must have a father,' she said.
'It'll have a father,' I said, 'we just won't be married. It's quite normal.'

AUTHORITY (CHRIS) Preparation for childbirth today is both a mental and a physical process. There are many different approaches, but they all aim to help mother and baby share the unique experience of birth.

ELIZABETH The first year of our marriage was great. We did everything together: talk, bed, work. Then I got pregnant. I didn't want a child. Not yet. Gerald wanted a child. Gerald wanted a son. (*To* GERALD) I'm the one who's pregnant, and I don't want it.

GERALD Okay. You pay for it.

ELIZABETH How?

GERALD   That's your problem. You raise the money and you can have your abortion.

AUTHORITY (CHRIS)   There is still much we do not know about the relationship between the mother's state of mind and that of her unborn child. But we do know that a happy and contented pregnancy and a good normal birth are very likely to produce a happy mother and hence the basis for a normal family life.

SUE   I've always liked women more than men. When I was younger, I had this idea that if I got married and had kids, like all my friends, I'd get over it. Then I met Peter. We got on really well. So when he asked me to marry him, I said 'Yes'.

CAROL   When I told my Mum I thought I was pregnant, she went right out and booked the church and the hall for the reception. We would have got married sooner or later. Nick said so. Julie was my first. I can hardly remember her birth — I was all drugged up on something or other. With Alex, I didn't need anything. With Julie, we hung my wedding ring on a piece of string over my stomach. It went round in a circle so we knew it would be a girl. It did the same with Alex — except he was a boy.

SARA   They didn't give up. The social worker tried to persuade me to have it adopted. I just laughed. She could see she wasn't getting very far with me, so we had a cigarette together.

ELIZABETH   I got toxaemia in the seventh month. My legs and hands swelled. I couldn't stand Gerald near me. I spent the last seven weeks in hospital.

SARA   When you're really big you can't get your tights up over your belly any more. I liked making love all the way through. I was an eggplant, an ocean liner.

AUTHORITY (MALE)   Scientific and humane.

AUTHORITY (CHRIS)   When the cervix is fully dilated, the mother will be allowed to follow her instincts and push down with each contraction. Breathe.

The cast breathe in unison.

Breathe deeply. This is it. Push, mother, push now.

Music rises to chords. Slides of the actual birth of a baby.

CAROL   Alex just shot out.

SARA   It was like a really good crap.

ELIZABETH   Forty-eight hours' labour.

Flute music.

AUTHORITY (CHRIS)   After baby is born, the mother has no further part to play, but can lie back and enjoy the fruits of her labour. The sooner she is able to do this, the quicker will the placenta (the afterbirth) come away. After the umbilical cord is cut, baby will be wrapped and given to mother.

STEPHEN   Oh, Sara, look how tiny she is. She looks just like you.

ELIZABETH   Dan was in an incubator for four days. They didn't know how much I needed to see him. Gerald saw him. He was glad it was a boy.

CAROL   It's nice having a girl and a boy.

AUTHORITY (CHRIS)   After the birth, mother will usually feel elated, and quite probably very hungry and thirsty as well.

ELIZABETH   I hardly slept for months. I used to scream at myself in the bathroom mirror. They told me I had post-natal depression. I said, 'Why didn't you warn me about it before?' I still couldn't stand Gerald near me.

CAROL   When Alex was six months old, I saw myself in a shop window one day. I looked really old. With a baby and a toddler you don't have a minute's peace. You're on duty the whole time. Nick had to do overtime; we hardly saw each other, and when we did, we never said more than three words.

SUE   Peter and I are okay. He accepts me for what I am. Lennie, our son, he's eight now. He's a smashing kid. I haven't stopped feeling the way I did about women. I was wrong about that. Still, you have to build your life as best you can. Being a mother hasn't changed me that much.

All but SARA *exit.*

Slides of SARA *bathing her baby, Lisa. Music: 'Nightsong.'*

SARA   (*brings on a clothes-horse and sets it behind the cushions, draping baby clothes over it*) Lisa was the most perfect thing I ever saw. I used to watch her sleeping at night, watch her breathing. I didn't open a book for three months. I was tired; I didn't sleep much. I cried. I cried all the time. I loved crying. I loved everything. Lisa was the most beautiful thing I ever made. I liked planning ahead most. When we'd go to the park, and I'd show her all my favourite things, the swings, ponies. I'd teach her to swim. All the things I loved I could do all over again with Lisa.

Scene Two

> SARA *lounges on the cushions, reading.* STEPHEN *enters, carrying a large shoulder-bag.*

SARA Well. You've come home.

STEPHEN I'm sorry.

SARA I'm sorry.

STEPHEN We're both sorry. Lisa asleep?

SARA Yes. I didn't mean you to walk out.

STEPHEN I didn't want to walk out.

SARA Don't go away again, alright? I said a lot of bullshit.

STEPHEN Yes.

SARA Well, maybe it wasn't all bullshit.

STEPHEN I just got upset. I'm so worried about these exams. Why am I so worried?

SARA Because there aren't many jobs and even fewer grants. The people you're competing with don't have to be tied down with babies and nappies and baby-sitting.

STEPHEN I don't feel tied down.

SARA I do. And you do too. It's no mystery. We are.

STEPHEN But I don't, I really don't —

SARA I'm not accusing you. I'm just saying it's tricky. The people we're at college with — the same people we'll be competing against for jobs — they don't have babies. So we're worried.

STEPHEN It's not that I don't love Lisa, it's not that I don't care about you or how your work is going —

SARA It's just that when you worry all you can see is how important your work is.

STEPHEN I do want you to do well.

SARA I actually did some work tonight. I opened a book and read and took notes — with a bit more time I'll even finish my essay. And I didn't jump up to listen for Lisa once. It is possible.

STEPHEN It is possible.

SARA Did you know that the Jews are the only people in the United Kingdom who can get married in their own homes without a special dispensation from the Archbishop of Canterbury?

STEPHEN What?

SARA Everyone else who pays rates has to do it in a registry office — at least, according to my 1967 sociology textbook. Look, we'll be okay. You'll get your grant and I'll finish my year. All that and a baby too — see, I like you.

STEPHEN   I missed you.

SARA   I love you.

STEPHEN   Did you miss me last night?

SARA   (*agreeing*) Mm hm. Except that I slept on the side of the bed that I like.

STEPHEN   My side?

SARA   That's right. Did you sleep last night? (STEPHEN *doesn't answer*) You did!

STEPHEN   If you can call sleeping on John's camp-bed sleeping. Hey, I got you a present. (*He gets a musical toy out of his bag*) Look.

SARA   Did you get me a dummy to go with it? No, it's just what I've always wanted.

STEPHEN   I'll hang it over Lisa's cot tonight and then when she wakes up she'll pull it to bits like she pulls everything to bits — (*He pulls the cord and the toy makes a noise*) — and she'll be so knocked out she won't want us to go in to her.

SARA   And you can lie in.

STEPHEN   And you can lie in.

SARA   So there we are, at six o'clock in the morning, listening to — (*She mimics the toy*) No, no, I like it.

STEPHEN   No, silly. There we are, lying in bed, you all warm and sleepy and instead of rushing off to get Lisa her bottle, we'll be — (*He whispers in her ear*)

SARA   (*turns away*) Oh, I'm sorry. It's just that when you walked out I thought you'd gone for good. I thought, what am I going to do? I can't finish my degree because I can't afford it, and I'm the only person in the world who'll hear Lisa when she cries. I thought, what if Lisa has a father who just pisses off all over the place, a father who's a pig? I didn't even think, 'Vicious bastard, he walked out.' I thought, 'He just walked out, what the hell am I going to do?'

STEPHEN   I wouldn't walk out, Sara.

SARA   But you did, Stephen. You could again. We're not married.

STEPHEN   I couldn't stay away.

SARA   But you did.

STEPHEN   I came back. You could walk out after a row, just the same as me.

SARA   I couldn't. I couldn't be five minutes away and not have my head back here. I feel so connected, it's like being on the end of a tight piece of elastic.

STEPHEN   I won't disappear; I promise.

SARA   I know. 'Cause I'd ring your parents up and set them on your trail. You don't know what your into.

STEPHEN   Oh, I'm beginning to.

SARA   Alright, where were you today?

STEPHEN   In the library.

SARA   You cheeky bastard, you worked.

STEPHEN   You worked too.

SARA   I've done an hour and a half tonight. I haven't caught up.

STEPHEN   Didn't you go to lectures?

SARA   How could I? I couldn't leave the house.

STEPHEN   Why didn't you take her to the baby-minder?

SARA   (*gets up and begins to fold the baby clothes*) I'm not going to use her any more.

STEPHEN   Why on earth not?

SARA   Stephen, she just piles Lisa up on the couch with three layers of nappies for the whole day. A baby hasn't crawled across her carpet for years. We'll have to find someone else.

STEPHEN   Isn't she registered?

SARA   Yes, but I can't even talk to her. I can't very well go to the council behind her back.

STEPHEN   I suppose she can't earn money any other way.

SARA   Maybe. But I can't afford sympathy for her when I'm scared of what's going to happen to Lisa. I can't very well say to her, 'Please love my baby like I do for 15p an hour.'

STEPHEN   But we haven't got any option. Lisa's too little to get into a nursery. We have to have a minder.

SARA   We'll do it between us. We'll do shifts — every other day, and we'll get our work done.

STEPHEN   It doesn't leave much time for so-called leisure.

SARA   Well, that's the way it's going to be.

STEPHEN   Look, let's go down to the town hall and see their list of baby-minders —

SARA   Alright, but if we can't find someone I like, we'll do it between us, alright?

STEPHEN   Let's try and find someone first, love.

SARA   Alright.

They exit, taking the baby clothes and clothes-horse.

Scene Three

Piano and flute music: 'Swings and Things.' Slides of SUE, CAROL, *Julie and Alex in the park.*

CAROL *and* SUE *run on, playing football,* CAROL *carrying a basket.*

CAROL   (*calls off*)   Julie, don't throw sand around.

SUE *scores.*

SUE   Goal!

CAROL   It was not.

SUE   It was too.

CAROL   Cheat. It's still two-one to me. (*They go on playing*) Here, that woman's watching us.

SUE   She probably thinks we nicked the football from some kid.

CAROL   No, look, hey, doesn't she look like Mrs Parker, she's the spitting image of Mrs Parker.

SUE   Don't be daft, Carol. Mrs Parker hasn't been out of bed for three years.

CAROL   She's still staring.

SUE   Watch. (*Calls off*) Lennie, give Julie her bucket and spade back. See? We're just a couple of Mums playing football. (*She shoots the ball*) Goal!

CAROL   Foul.

SUE   Free kick to me.

CAROL   Alright, indirect. Get back. (SUE *dances from side to side.*) What are you doing?

SUE   Building a wall.

CAROL   Forming a wall. Don't you ever watch tele?

SUE   Alright, forming a wall. (*She closes in on* CAROL *and they scuffle round the ball*) Hey, if this week's no good, what about next Wednesday?

CAROL   Nick's on night shift all week.

SUE   Great. Shall I bring some wine?

CAROL   You sure you can get away?

SUE   Of course. If Peter's out I'll take Lennie next door. She won't mind looking after him. I'll tell her I've got an extra sleeping-in duty to do.

CAROL   Tell her Mrs Parker wants to watch a horror movie and she needs you to hold her hand. I feel really sorry for Mrs Parker.

SUE   What do you mean? She's got wonderful people like us looking after her.

CAROL   Yes, but ending up in an old folks' home — (*She shoots a goal*) Goal. Match-of-the-day shot, if ever I saw one.

SUE   Shit.

CAROL   What's wrong?

SUE   My bloody ankle. I think I ricked it.

CAROL   (*pretends to blow whistle*) Injury time. (*She helps* SUE *over to the 'bench'*) Carefully, you cost us fifty thousand. Right. (*She looks at the ankle*) It's not swollen. Shall I strap it up?

SUE   It's alright.

CAROL   (*rubs the ankle*) That better?

SUE   Lovely.

CAROL   Here, she's still watching us.

SUE   Don't be silly. The park's full of women with kids.

CAROL   I wonder if they're having affairs too? Wouldn't that be funny.

SUE   That's what I like about the park. We can just be together and it doesn't matter.

CAROL   I wish we could have more time together. Properly. Without having to worry about anything.

SUE   We will. We'll have the whole night together next Wednesday.

CAROL   Don't forget to bring your alarm clock.

SUE   Oh, God.

CAROL   I'm always afraid we're going to sleep through both alarms and Nick's going to come in.

SUE   Put it in a biscuit tin.

CAROL   What?

SUE   The alarms. We'll put them in a biscuit tin.

CAROL   I'm worried about Nick.

SUE   Look, how's Nick going to find out?

CAROL   I don't know. I mean, what if someone saw us and what if someone made a joke and what if Nick heard and what if Nick realised?

SUE   What if, what if, what if? Carol, you're worrying about nothing. The only way he'll find out is if we tell him.

CAROL   But what if he went on strike and had to come home?

SUE   In the middle of the night? Come on, you're getting paranoid. We're not going to rob a bank, you know.

CAROL   Pity. We could do with the money. Hey, I must go, I haven't got Nick's tea yet.

CAROL *and* SUE *get ready to go.*

SUE   Wednesday — shall I come round about nine?

CAROL   Look, wait in the pub at the bottom of my road, just in case anything goes wrong.

SUE   Okay. If you're not there by nine-thirty, I'll know it's alright.

CAROL   Right. (*Calls*) Lennie, come on, we're going home.

SUE   (*calls*) Don't forget the push-chair, Julie.

They exit to music: 'Swings and Things'.

———

Scene Four

CHRIS *is seated at the table, looking through conference papers.* ELIZABETH *brings in coffee and biscuits.*

ELIZABETH   What a day.

CHRIS   Dan asleep?

ELIZABETH   Nearly. He had a great time. Thanks for the lift.

CHRIS   That's alright. Actually, I can't stay. I've got all the disco equipment in the van. Do you think you'll make it tomorrow?

ELIZABETH   I'd like to go to the discussion on the nursery campaign, but it may be a bit much for Dan. I'll see.

CHRIS   It'd be really nice if you did.

GERALD *enters.*

ELIZABETH   Gerald. Chris, this is Gerald, my husband.

CHRIS   Hello.

GERALD   How do you do. I don't believe we've met before.

ELIZABETH   You're home early.

GERALD   Yes. I phoned you earlier. Where have you been all day?

ELIZABETH   At the conference. I told you last week.

GERALD　Oh. (*To* CHRIS) Are you in this Women's Lib thing?

CHRIS·　Liberation. Yes, I am.

GERALD　Elizabeth's been taking quite an interest in this — ah, Women's Liberation. Of course, it's very useful for her work, digging up facts about social injustice for the radio, but never actually getting her hands dirty with real life.

ELIZABETH　Please, Gerald, let's not have a row in front of Chris.

GERALD　No, of course not. Where's Dan?

ELIZABETH　Asleep.

GERALD　Where's he been all day?

ELIZABETH　At the creche.

GERALD　You took Dan to this women's conference?

CHRIS　He liked the creche. It was run by men.

GERALD　Really? Ah. (*To* CHRIS) You married?

CHRIS　No.

GERALD　Ah. Not married. Don't believe in it?

CHRIS　No, I don't actually.

ELIZABETH　Don't let him give you the third degree, Chris.

CHRIS　It's alright. Gerald — if you're not doing anything tomorrow, you could come and help in the creche.

GERALD　The what?

CHRIS　The creche. Nursery.

GERALD　Sunday's Sunday. If I wanted to look after other people's kids I'd be a headmaster, wouldn't I?

ELIZABETH　(*to* CHRIS) More coffee?

CHRIS　No, really, I must go. Will I see you tomorrow?

ELIZABETH　I hope so.

CHRIS　(*to* GERALD) Goodnight. (*She leaves*)

GERALD　(*looking at the papers*) What's all this, then?

ELIZABETH　Literature.

GERALD　I see. Did you tell me you were going to this conference?

ELIZABETH　Yes, I did. And I asked you to have Dan for the day and you said you couldn't, you were going on a sales trip.

GERALD　Funny. I don't remember it.

ELIZABETH　I'm tired. I'm going to bed.

GERALD Not even a shared cup of coffee before we retire to our respective bedrooms?

ELIZABETH Do you want some coffee?

GERALD I wouldn't say no. I wouldn't say no to a speaking relationship, like we used to have. You seemed to be having quite a cosy little chat when I came in. I was quite surprised to find someone in my kitchen at this hour of the night.

ELIZABETH It's only nine o'clock. Do you want a coffee or not?

GERALD This conference. What happens at this conference?

ELIZABETH (*indicates papers*) There.

GERALD How many people there?

ELIZABETH About fifteen hundred women.

GERALD This friend of yours — Chris — you known her long?

ELIZABETH A while

GERALD Her hair's very short.

ELIZABETH Lots of women have very short hair, Gerald.

GERALD Lots of women at this conference?

ELIZABETH Yes. *And* in the Sunday colour supplements.

GERALD Her clothes are a bit informal.

ELIZABETH Comfortable.

GERALD Where did you meet her?

ELIZABETH She came to speak to my group one evening.

GERALD Ah, yes, that weekly coven. You know, I've never minded you going to those women's meetings.

ELIZABETH Thank you.

GERALD Actually, I thought it was good you had an interest.

ELIZABETH Don't patronise me, Gerald. Don't pretend you haven't been hostile to the whole thing.

GERALD You're quite wrong, Elizabeth. If anyone has become more unpleasant and aggressive over the past months, it's certainly been you. Let's not pretend that these new friends of yours haven't had any bearing on the situation here at home.

ELIZABETH Gerald, don't think I haven't got a mind of my own.

GERALD I'm not saying that. I'm merely saying that we're all open to stimulation.

ELIZABETH That's right.

GERALD And this Chris — you find her stimulating?

ELIZABETH   Yes. I enjoy being with her.

GERALD   You enjoy *being* with her? Being *with* her?

ELIZABETH   Yes.

GERALD   Being with her, or talking with her?

ELIZABETH   You work that one out.

GERALD   You used the words 'being with her'.

ELIZABETH   Oh, Gerald, you know what I mean — talking with her, enjoying her company. I enjoy women's company.

GERALD   I enjoy men's company.

ELIZABETH   Well, good.

GERALD   A drink, a chat . . . have you been talking to her about us?

ELIZABETH   It's my business what I talk about with my friends. I'm going to bed.

GERALD   I'm trying to have a discussion.

ELIZABETH   The only thing I want to discuss with you is the divorce. There's no point in talking. No point in dragging on and on and dragging each other down. It's been going on for months.

GERALD   That's not true.

ELIZABETH   Do you really enjoy co-existing in the house like this — and you occasionally make me sleep with you. I don't want that sort of wordless sex. I don't even feel emotion about it any more.

GERALD   I'm only trying to help you.

ELIZABETH   You're not helping me. We're not helping each other.

GERALD   You enjoy a full relationship with me.

ELIZABETH   Do you think I enjoy being screwed by you?

GERALD   You have.

ELIZABETH   You're living in the past. I'm going.

GERALD   (*obstructs her*) You do enjoy it, you do.

ELIZABETH   Let me go, Gerald.

GERALD   Other women find me attractive.

ELIZABETH   I don't want to —

GERALD   I want to know about you.

ELIZABETH   I don't want to hear any more about me — just get it through your head, Gerald, I'm not going to change my mind.

GERALD   I'm not trying to change your mind.

ELIZABETH   Then leave me alone. I'm not going to dis —

GERALD   I disgust you in bed, right?

ELIZABETH   Yes, you do.

GERALD   And other men?

ELIZABETH   I haven't been with other men.

GERALD   You don't need — fulfilment?

ELIZABETH   At the moment, no. Not from you.

GERALD   From other men?

ELIZABETH   Oh, Gerald.

GERALD   Some of the women — in this group — it's clear that some of the women in the Women's Liberation — they're not interested in men in any way, right?

ELIZABETH   Their sexual choice has got nothing to do with you.

GERALD   They're obviously having an influence on you. I'm not unaware that you have some special relationship with this Chris, this girl.

ELIZABETH   Woman. We are friends.

GERALD   What does that mean?

ELIZABETH   What do you think 'friend' means?

GERALD   Well, if you both dislike men? Does Chris dislike men?

ELIZABETH   I don't know.

GERALD   You must know. She's your friend.

ELIZABETH   We never discuss men in that way. It's none of your business.

GERALD   Of course it's my business. I'm your husband. If you're going through some psychological disorder, I have a right to know. What exactly do you want? Is it this Chris woman?

ELIZABETH   I want to go to bed.

GERALD   Look, I won't be here much longer.

ELIZABETH   Good. When are you going.

GERALD   When I'm fucking well ready. It's still my house.

ELIZABETH   Just get out of my way.

GERALD   I'm still your husband, I still have rights. (*He grabs her*) I disgust you, do I? Tell me, what doesn't disgust you? Abortion, that doesn't disgust you?

ELIZABETH   No, it doesn't. Let me go.

They struggle and GERALD *pushes her down onto the cushions.*

GERALD   I don't want to hurt you . . .

Music: 'Checkmate'. Slides of ELIZABETH *in her dressing-gown, having breakfast with* DAN, *then* ELIZABETH *alone in her kitchen.*

Scene Five

CAROL *brings on a blanket and some cushions and lounges on the boxes, listening to a French tape, repeating odd phrases after it.*

SUE *comes in.*

CAROL   What did she want, cherie?

SUE   She wanted another pill to make her go. If she had her way she'd be sitting on the commode all day. It's like Brands Hatch up there.

CAROL   Did you bring down Mrs Harrington's tray?

SUE   Damn, I forgot. I'll get it in the morning when the teas go up. I think everything's okay now. (*She sits beside* CAROL)

CAROL   So. Comment ca va, Madame Harris?

SUE   Very well thanks, Mrs Denver. (*They kiss*)

CAROL   Ooh la la. And if Mrs Stuart walks in I'll say, 'Oh, my goodness, Mrs Harris has fainted — (SUE *joins in*) — and I was giving her the kiss of life!

SUE   I forgot to tell you — I didn't take the alarm clock out of my bag this morning.

CAROL   Did he notice?

SUE   It rang — right in the middle of breakfast.

CAROL   Did he say anything?

SUE   Well, Peter asked me what it was doing in my bag.

CAROL   You took it shopping with you. You're a rotten liar. What did you say?

SUE   I said something about my watch being broken.

CAROL   So you strapped the alarm clock to your wrist?

SUE   Don't be ridiculous. He didn't believe me, of course. He said it was a fine carry-on and didn't I think I was being rather silly, carrying an alarm clock round with me.

CAROL   What did you say?

SUE   What could I say? I just sort of ummed and aahed . . .

CAROL   What did he say?

SUE   He said, 'You're in love with her, aren't you?'

CAROL   Oh, no.

SUE   He's not an idiot, you know. Anyway, he's right, isn't he? Long live honesty.

CAROL   Jesus, any more honesty floating around and I'm dead. I'm not joking, Sue. Nick would kill me if he found out.

SUE   How's he going to find out? He doesn't even know Peter. Look, you're going to have to say something, sometime.

CAROL   No.

SUE   Carol, you're having an affair with a woman, a lesbian affair.

CAROL   Oh, leave off. Why do you have to start talking rubbish every time we're alone together?

SUE   I'm sorry. (*Pause*) Have you started packing for your holidays yet?

CAROL   No. The kids have started. They're taking everything, buckets, spades, everything.

SUE   Sounds like Lennie.

CAROL   Oh, Julie wants to send Lennie a postcard. Will you write to me?

SUE   You're the one who's going on holiday. You do the writing.

CAROL   I will — when no one's looking.

SUE   And what about when they are? What are you going to do with yourself for two weeks?

CAROL   Sit on the sands, listen to my French tapes.

SUE   They speak a lot of French in Skegness, do they?

CAROL   Not so's you'd notice.

SUE   How are you getting there?

CAROL   Train.

SUE   Sleeper?

CAROL   No.

SUE   Too cosy?

CAROL   Too expensive. I'll miss you, Sue.

SUE   Taking any fancy dresses?

CAROL   Probably. I'll need at least one while we're away.

SUE   Which dress? Your Laura Ashley?

CAROL   I don't know.

SUE   Jesus. You don't have to jump down my throat.

CAROL   What a stupid question. Of course I'll take at least one nice dress.

SUE   I don't care. I was just asking.

CAROL   I might even have my hair done. I may even lie around on the beach enjoying myself. That alright?

SUE   Fine.

CAROL   Christ.

SUE   Whatever turns you on.

CAROL   What turns me on is you, but you don't want to listen so I may as well not bother.

SUE   Carol . . . I do . . .

CAROL   All you can see is me going on holiday with Nick. And you can't take it. Well, there's nothing I can do about it.

SUE   You could if you really wanted to.

CAROL   Like what?

SUE   Like not go.

CAROL   We go away every year, Sue, it's been booked ages.

SUE   And what about me?

CAROL   What do you mean, what about you? You want to come too?

SUE   Me stuck here while you're off with your husband.

CAROL   You'll be with your husband.

SUE   Yes, but if I didn't want to go away on holiday with Peter I bloody wouldn't go.

CAROL   It's alright for you, isn't it? Peter knows about you. He doesn't even care. Anyway, he's off with Stella. Nick doesn't know about me.

SUE   Well, tell him.

CAROL   I can't.

SUE   If we're really serious you'll have to tell him. You want to go on holiday with Nick, don't you?

CAROL   If that's what you want to believe . . .

SUE   Bloody hell. I'm tired of sneaking out of your bed at five a.m. so that Nick can crawl in at eight. I just don't think I can cope with it for much longer.

CAROL   Do you think I like it?

SUE   I don't know where you're at at all. I think we'd better forget the whole thing.

CAROL   Sue, I can't forget it, you know that. I love you.

SUE   Big deal.

CAROL   I won't stop seeing you. I'll keep ringing you up.

SUE   What could you say? I think you're just stringing me along while you're working things out. While you wait sixteen years for your kids to grow up or fifty years till Nick drops dead.

CAROL   I'm not stringing you along. It isn't that simple.

SUE   Of course it bloody isn't.

CAROL   Look, I can't just choose between you and Nick, if that's what you want. I can't walk out with no money and nowhere to take the kids. If you really want to know, I'm scared stiff of walking out. What do you want me to do?

SUE   I don't know. I expect you'll make up your mind and let me know. Right? I'll go and check on Mrs Lewis.

SUE *exits. Music: slow phrase of 'Swings and Things'.*   CAROL *exits with blanket and cushions. She leaves the radio cassette onstage.*

———————

Scene Six

Music: 'Nightsong'. STEPHEN *enters and sits at the table, working at his books.* SARA *enters, takes off her coat and sits on the cushions.*

SARA   Have you eaten?

STEPHEN   Yes.

SARA   Have you done a lot of work?

STEPHEN   Quite a lot.

SARA   What, with Lisa around?

STEPHEN   She's no problem. She was playing with a bowl of cornflakes.

SARA   Cornflakes?

STEPHEN   Yes. Crackling them, crunching them, chucking them around. Very happy, she was. I just worked.

SARA   Chucking them around — on the floor — in the kitchen?

STEPHEN   I cleaned up. (SARA *gets up*) Where are you going?

SARA   To make sure it's really clean.

STEPHEN   Oh, leave it.

SARA   Somebody's got to care. (*She sits at the table*)

STEPHEN   Isn't the course going well?

SARA   I'd just as soon stay at home and paint the flat sometimes.

STEPHEN   Well, you can.

SARA   I don't want to. It's just that — all the time I'm working I have this sort of parallel track of thought, thinking about what you're doing at the same time.

STEPHEN   That's ridiculous. You can't live your life only in relation to me. Anyway, aren't things better, now I'm helping you more with Lisa? You don't want to spend all your time looking after us — you said so.

SARA   I feel as though I'm the glue that keeps us all together.

STEPHEN   We don't stay together because we're stuck to each other, do we?

SARA   I don't know.

STEPHEN   So what is it?

SARA   Some sort of duty, maybe. I want us to be *really* together, that's what I want.

STEPHEN   We are. I can't see the problem.

SARA   Well, what's going to happen in the next five years?

STEPHEN   Five-year plan, eh?

SARA   What will you do when you get your MA?

STEPHEN   I don't know. I'll find something.

SARA   You see — there's one difference between us. I can't just say I don't know what I'll do when I get my degree. I mean, certain decisions have already been made for me. I can't live where there are damp walls. I have to live where there's a decent school. I have all these conditions built round me, and at the same time I have to leave myself open so that what you want to do can fit into the picture.

STEPHEN   Aren't you happy?

SARA   I don't know. I'm just telling you what's going on.

STEPHEN   Sara — Tim suggested today that you and me and Lisa move into Ken and Alice's place. What do you think?

SARA   What do you think?

STEPHEN   Well, we have to admit it just isn't working out. We're not like we used to be, we're just not getting on well any more. And it'd be far easier with Lisa with other people around.

SARA   You mean they'd all babysit?

STEPHEN   They'd help, I'm sure.

SARA   Did Tim say they'd help?

STEPHEN   Well, no, not —

SARA   I'd be bitching at four people instead of just you.

STEPHEN   It's not a question of bitching. If we lived with other people we would all have to share responsibility, and then we'd both have more time. That's what we want, isn't it?

SARA   I can see what's supposed to happen, I just don't see it happening. I don't know how to say this — I feel you want to use this house as a way of dropping your responsibilities to me and Lisa. I think your next step will be straight out through the door. I do.

STEPHEN   It's an opportunity to try a new kind of life.

SARA   Stephen, they're all graduate students, they've got no time to look after people. It'll just be a token feather in their cap to have a baby in the house. Look how groovy we are.

STEPHEN   Sara, I can't finish my thesis like this. Lisa can't get into nursery till she's two. I can't mark time for a year. Our time is always at the expense of each other's.

SARA   I have this picture of us all sitting round the table eating brown rice and passing the carrot juice, and I'm the one who jumps up and down like a jack in the box to see to Lisa.

STEPHEN   You're always looking for ways of making a martyr of yourself.

SARA   I'm not trying to be a martyr. I have certain instincts. It's not my fault. I care about the quality of time spent with Lisa. If someone is reading her a book, they're not just trying to teach her words, but concepts. She's not a dog that you just put in a kennel.

STEPHEN   You're not the only one who cares about her development.

SARA   I would love it if other people really did care. If there was the sort of social responsibility towards babies and toddlers that there is towards schoolkids.

STEPHEN   You're just being paranoid.

SARA   But you've said yourself, you don't like the responsibility.

STEPHEN   It's not that. It needn't be so heavy.

SARA   You want out, don't you? Why can't you come straight out with it? All this alternative stuff is bullshit. You have to be rich to have an alternative.

STEPHEN   Alright, how would you feel if I said I couldn't stand all this any more?

SARA   Like I do now. Blown apart.

STEPHEN   We'll explode if we stay together here.

SARA   Stephen, these years are important for Lisa. I want someone who's connected to Lisa, not a whole lot of people who'll piss off whenever they feel like it.

STEPHEN   For someone who's opposed to marriage you cling bloody hard to its principles.

SARA   I don't want to be married. I don't want to feel this clinging feeling —

STEPHEN   Look, I could move in there now, give you some more time to think about it. I could go and tell them now.

SARA   Are you going to pay for both places? I can't afford this place on my own.

STEPHEN   Well, then, move in with us.

SARA   So you're saying that if I want financial security, I have to follow you around.

STEPHEN   I'm giving you the choice.

SARA   You're giving me nothing. You've already said yes to them, haven't you?

STEPHEN   I can afford it on my own.

SARA   I see. And what am I supposed to do about me and Lisa?

STEPHEN   You've got your grant.

SARA   Look, mate. Your name's on that birth certificate. Now you can leave, but you're not going to stop supporting your daughter. And as I want to live with her and look after her, I'll need money. Stephen, I could move into a commune if we had a strong relationship or even if I was on my own, but I won't move into a commune with a disintegrating relationship.

STEPHEN   You're making it very difficult.

SARA   Yes, I am. I'm the one who says rent has to be paid, food costs money. I can't support two of us on my grant.

STEPHEN   Then you'll just have to get Social Security, won't you.

SARA   Piss off out of it, then. Leave me alone.

STEPHEN   You're scared, really, aren't you? Well, you can stay put, but don't try and stop me from moving on.

SARA   You're not talking about change, choice or anything that you and your friends can give me. You're so short-sighted you can't see what's making me so insecure, making me want something like a marriage. I've got to survive; that's what women do in this world. That's why they get so upset when someone says 'I'm sorry, I don't love you any more.'

STEPHEN   How can you want all this?

He exits. SARA *watches him go, then collects her coat and exits.*

———

Scene Seven

> SUE *is standing waiting for* CAROL *in a pub. She holds a glass.* CAROL *enters in a hurry.*

CAROL Sue, I told Nick. We'd been getting on alright on holiday, started talking about a lot of things. I thought if I told him about us we could talk about that too. I must have been crazy.

SUE What did he say?

CAROL He hit me. He called me a filthy lesbian and a pervert. It was awful. Everyone in the flats must know by now. The kids were screaming and Julie was crying, and then the woman upstairs came down and said she was going to call the police if we didn't pack it in. Old cow.

SUE So what happened?

CAROL In the end Nick went out and I took the kids round to me Mum's. He'll be pissed out of his head when he gets back.

SUE You can't go back tonight.

CAROL I'm not going back ever. Before he went he said, he got hold of me like that, and he said, 'Either you give up that job and never see that woman again or any other women friends and stay home and look after me, or I'm getting a divorce.' What a thing to say to someone.

SUE What are you going to do?

CAROL I'm leaving him. I'm not going to be locked up like a prisoner in my own home.

SUE Oh, Carol.

CAROL Even if it wasn't for you, I wouldn't stay with him now.

SUE Jesus, what a turn-up.

CAROL Mum was great. She said if Nick comes round she'll belt him with a frying pan. I'll have to look for a flat.

SUE Carol — can you afford a flat on your own?

CAROL I don't know. I haven't thought properly. Will you help me look?

SUE We could look for a flat together. Have you thought?

CAROL No. No, I didn't. What, now, you and me? What about Peter?

SUE Well, while you were away, Peter and me also did a bit of talking. He and Stella want to live together, so we'll have to get divorced. I may as well leave now, then you and me could look for somewhere together.

CAROL Sue, do you mean that?

SUE 'Course I do. That row before you went on holiday wasn't just hot air, you know.

CAROL   We'll have to start looking at ads in the paper. I want to move right away from Dagenham. Do you mind?

SUE   Of course not.

CAROL   We'll have to get new jobs —

SUE   Schools for the kids —

CAROL   You'll bring Lennie, won't you?

SUE   Of course I will.

CAROL   What about Peter?

SUE   Him and me'll sort that out. Come on, I'll drive you back to your Mum's.

———

Scene Eight

> *Slides of* CHRIS, ELIZABETH, *and* DAN *having a day out. Music: 'Funday'.* CHRIS *comes on, and unpacks a carrier bag. She finds a toy plastic gun.*

ELIZABETH   (*calls off as she enters*) Put your pyjamas on, love. I'll come up and say goodnight. And Chris.

CHRIS   Look.

ELIZABETH   Where was that?

CHRIS   Under the teabags.

ELIZABETH   He must have picked it up on the boat.

CHRIS   Yes. I don't really approve of taking kids round warships.

ELIZABETH   The Cutty Sark wasn't a warship, it was a tea-clipper.

CHRIS   Even worse. That's British Imperialism at its height. What shall I do with it?

ELIZABETH   Oh, he might as well keep it. He's always nagging me for guns.

CHRIS   That reminds me: what shall I get him for his birthday? We've got some new books in the bookshop.

ELIZABETH   He's a bit young for the *Dialectics of Sex*.

CHRIS   Oh, very funny. How about *Noddy and Big Ears*?

ELIZABETH   He's better off with the gun.

> GERALD *saunters in.*

ELIZABETH   Gerald.

GERALD   She remembers my name. Well, hello there, girls.

ELIZABETH   Where did you come from?

GERALD   Through the front door. I've been here quite some time.

ELIZABETH   Why didn't you tell me you were coming? Sneaking round the house like that.

GERALD   Who's sneaking. I've come to see Dan. So. How's my ex-wife? Still got your funny friends, I see.

CHRIS   I beg your pardon.

GERALD   I'd like to talk to you privately. Would you ask your friend to leave.

ELIZABETH   No.

GERALD   Dan was pleased to see me. I went up and kissed him goodnight. I suppose you forgot about him, sitting here, gossiping with your friend.

ELIZABETH   What do you want?

GERALD   I want to talk about Dan. I don't discuss my son in front of strange women.

ELIZABETH   Chris isn't a stranger.

GERALD   That is very obvious. You can tell what she is just by looking at her.

CHRIS   So?

GERALD   I'm asking you quite civilly to leave.

ELIZABETH   She's my guest and she's staying.

GERALD   I could call the police and have you forcibly removed.

CHRIS   You could, if you don't mind making a fool of yourself. (*To* ELIZABETH) Shall I go up and say goodnight to Dan?

GERALD   Don't you go near Dan. He's my son, remember? I don't want you to have any more to do with him. I don't want you taking him anywhere, giving him presents. Is that clear?

ELIZABETH   Chris, you don't have to listen to this.

CHRIS   (*moves towards* ELIZABETH) It's alright.

GERALD   Don't you touch her. Don't think that just because the divorce is final you can move in here and take my place. Do you enjoy stealing women from their husbands?

ELIZABETH   Don't shout. You'll disturb your son.

GERALD   (*to* CHRIS) Why don't you just get the fuck out of my house. I'll put your face through the bloody window, that's what I'll do.

ELIZABETH   That's enough. Chris, would you stay tonight?

GERALD   Do you think it's healthy for Dan to be sleeping in the same house as two bent women?

ELIZABETH   The bed's made up in the spare room. Gerald can see himself out.

GERALD   If she's staying, so am I. I shall stay here and make sure there's no creeping along the corridors.

CHRIS   Will you be okay, Elizabeth?

GERALD   Of course she'll be okay. I'm not going to rape her.

CHRIS   Surprise, surprise.

GERALD   What's that?

CHRIS   Nothing, nothing.

ELIZABETH   Goodnight, Chris. (CHRIS *exits*)

GERALD   I dread to think what the boy's heard already.

ELIZABETH   Keep your voice down. (*She exits*)

GERALD   And seen. (*He takes the radio, and turns it on, tuning it till he finds some music. He shouts over it*) Hey, you, staying the whole night, are you? Not going to be much fun for you, I'm afraid. Can't screw my wife tonight.

ELIZABETH   (*enters*) Will you shut up and turn that thing off.

GERALD   Just fuck off back to bed.

ELIZABETH *exits*.

What's so special about this woman, then? Hey, screwface, what's so special about you? What have you got that I haven't? What do you do to each other? Couldn't you make it as a real woman? You're worse than a whore. I can understand a whore. I'm not having my son living in a female brothel. Perverts. Lesbians, Dykes. (*To* ELIZABETH) I'll take you to court and then everyone will know you for what you are. The days Dan spends with you are coming to an end. I know too much about you. (*He picks up the gun, mock shoots in* ELIZABETH'*s direction and exits, leaving the radio blaring*)

ELIZABETH *and* CHRIS *enter from opposite sides.* ELIZABETH *turns the radio off.*

ELIZABETH   Chris, I'm really sorry—

CHRIS   You don't have to apologise, Elizabeth.

ELIZABETH   I couldn't believe how vicious he was.

CHRIS   Couldn't you? I could. Oh, I don't mean him specifically, just that kind of attitude. People do talk like that.

ELIZABETH   What, calling you names like that?

CHRIS It's not just the names. It's all that shit about not being a real woman, and couldn't I get a man. Mostly I can ignore it — but there's one thing that always gets to me.

ELIZABETH What?

CHRIS Someone using 'lesbian' as a term of abuse.

ELIZABETH I'm sorry.

CHRIS Look, don't —

ELIZABETH I'll change the lock.

CHRIS You'll have to do more than change the lock.

ELIZABETH Like?

CHRIS Get in touch with your solicitor.

ELIZABETH What, that stuff about going back to court? He was pissed.

CHRIS Well, you know him better than I do.

ELIZABETH He wouldn't. It's settled. I've got custody. He may hate me but it's settled.

CHRIS What if he appeals?

ELIZABETH Can he?

CHRIS Yes. He could say all those things about us in court. Claim you're an unfit mother because you've got lesbian friends.

ELIZABETH What? But he can't prove anything. There's nothing to prove.

CHRIS He doesn't need photographs. If he insinuates enough about us he may not find it that difficult to convince a court. Women still aren't supposed to be friends with each other, remember?

ELIZABETH Oh, God.

CHRIS I think you should talk to your solicitor. Just in case.

ELIZABETH Not the one I had for the divorce. I mean, that was all quite straightforward. I can't see him coping with this.

CHRIS Well, I know a feminist solicitor. You could talk to her.

ELIZABETH I don't think I can face having to deal with Gerald all over again.

CHRIS Elizabeth, if he appeals, you'll want to fight, won't you?

ELIZABETH I haven't got any choice.

———

Scene Nine

CAROL *is packing last-minute toys.* SUE *enters.*

SUE   Okay. The cases are all in the car. There's only this lot.

CAROL   Will there be enough room?

SUE   Oh, yes. (*She picks a toy up*) You won't want this. It's broken.

CAROL   I'll take it anyway.

SUE   What about the radio? Whose is it, yours or Nick's?

CAROL   Everything's Nick's. Leave it. I hope I've got everything.

SUE   Right. We'll get the kids from your Mum's and we're off. What have you told them?

CAROL   Just that we're all going to live together. They think it's another holiday. Is Lennie in the car?

SUE   No, he isn't.

CAROL   We'll pick him up on the way, then.

SUE   Carol, Lennie's not coming.

CAROL   What?

SUE   Lennie. He's staying here. Peter wants him to. There won't be any hassles about the divorce.

CAROL   Oh, no, Sue.

SUE   Well, perhaps it's the best thing for Lennie. He gets on really well with his Dad.

CAROL   He gets on really well with you. You can't let Peter do that.

SUE   It's not just Peter. We both decided.

CAROL   What does Lennie think?

SUE   He's eight, he's not a baby any more. Peter thinks that it would be better if Lennie stayed with him and Stella. More stable. It's not that he disapproves of us, just that it would be easier for Lennie. We've argued about it a lot. But he really loves Lennie.

CAROL   Why didn't you tell me before?

SUE   I didn't want to worry you. What with all the hassle of the last few weeks.

CAROL   If I'd known you were losing Lennie . . .

SUE   I'm not losing Lennie. Peter and I will have joint custody and he'll come to us at weekends and in the holidays. We've talked to Lennie about it and he's fine. He loves us both. Peter wouldn't let him be unhappy.

CAROL   Won't Peter change his mind?

SUE   No.

CAROL   Sue, if you don't want to come away now, I'll understand.

SUE   I do want to. I'll just have to get used to two kids instead of three, that's all.

CAROL   We're off, then?

SUE   Definitely.

CAROL   What about the key? What if I want to come back and get some more stuff? No, I'll leave it. That's Nick's too.

SUE   Right. Say ta-ta to the house.

CAROL   Ta-ta to the house.

They exit.

ACT TWO

The two boxes are placed downstage left and right; two chairs upstage centre, in front of the screen, facing the audience. All the cast, except CAROL *and* ELIZABETH, *wear identical red shirts and read from identical black folders when they are playing* AUTHORITY *figures. The actor/actress reading the various authority figures (who represent judge, lawyer, social workers, psychiatrists etc) is indicated for each speech.*

Music: 'Checkmate'. SARA *and* STEPHEN *enter and sit on box down right.* CAROL *enters and sits on box down left.* ELIZABETH *enters and stands.* SUE *and* CHRIS *enter,* SUE *stands in front of chair upstage left, and* CHRIS *stands in front of chair upstage right.*

Scene One

AUTHORITY (SUE)   Silence. Order in Court. Silence in Court. Read the charges. Present the petition.

AUTHORITY (CHRIS)   Most people in our society today can expect to marry at some time in their lives. Some may even experiment with the institution more than once. This is because, although the divorce rate has risen steadily in the last decade, so has the rate of remarriage by divorced partners.

AUTHORITY (SUE)   The family today is still the backbone of society. Where individuals cannot conform to its demands, judgement must be made.

STEPHEN *and* SARA *stand.*

AUTHORITY (CHRIS)   Do you swear that the evidence you shall give shall be the truth, the whole truth and nothing but the truth?

STEPHEN   I do.

SARA   I do.

Music stops. CHRIS *and* SUE *sit.*

————

Scene Two

STEPHEN   I'm sorry it's been such an ordeal for you.

SARA   You didn't come to visit Lisa for a year and a half.

STEPHEN   I don't think we should talk about it any more. We went through it all in there.

SARA   I just don't believe you've won.

STEPHEN   You have access. You can come and see her.

SARA   I'm going to see her right now. I'm going to have to explain to her why she's got to go away with complete strangers who don't know what she calls her toy animals.

STEPHEN   She's already been picked up, Sara.

SARA   She's what? Who's she with?

STEPHEN   Catherine.

SARA   Oh, my God. I've warned her against strangers. She'll think I've walked out on her.

STEPHEN   Surely it's best to make a clean break.

SARA   How did Catherine know you'd got custody? You had her on the hot line, waiting for the pickup.

STEPHEN   Sara, give Lisa a chance to settle in her new home.

SARA   What are you going to say to her?

STEPHEN   Catherine —

SARA   What are *you* going to tell her?

STEPHEN   Look, you can phone her tonight.

SARA   I'm supposed to phone her up and say 'Sorry, darling, I can't see you for a week'? She'll go nuts.

Music

AUTHORITY (CHRIS *stands*)   The father, aged twenty-five, is a lecturer at a polytechnic. The mother, aged twenty-three, is a copy-editor for a small publishing company. I would have thought, generally speaking, that a little girl of this age, three years old, would be better looked after by her mother, and there is no doubt that the mother has acquitted herself well.

However, we must think in terms of the child's future best interests. If the father were on his own, I would have no hesitation in refusing his application for custody. But since he and his new wife are more than prepared, as we have heard from the evidence, to provide a comfortable and loving home for Lisa, I will award him custody, care and control. Regular weekly access may be reasonably worked out between the two parties. (*She sits*).

Music stops.

SARA   Has Catherine ever taken a kid to the toilet? Lisa likes having a friend in the toilet with her.

STEPHEN   Catherine's dealt with children before.

SARA   Not my child.

STEPHEN   Believe me, I didn't want it to be —

SARA   How did you want it to be? Easy and nice? How was it going to be easy and nice, taking a kid away from me that I've brought up?

———

Scene Three

SARA   (*sits on box down right, facing audience*)   I'll believe society takes fatherhood seriously, when the Gents in the motorway services has a babies' changing room, just like the Ladies has.

AUTHORITY (CHRIS)   Guardianship of minors. Grant versus Grant. Appeal for custody and maintenance of minor, Daniel Grant.

ELIZABETH   I thought Gerald had accepted the terms of the divorce. I never thought he'd actually go through with an appeal for custody. (*She sits on the box down right, with her back to the audience.*)

AUTHORITY (CHRIS) Guardianship of minors, Denver versus Denver. Complaint for custody and maintenance of minors, Julie and Alexander Denver.

CAROL Maintenance? Nick's never paid me a penny.

SUE (*crosses to box down left and sits with* CAROL) No, look, he's applying for the kids — 'that the custody of the minors be granted to the complainant'.

CAROL He can't take the kids away. He hasn't been to see them more than three times since we moved. He's got no one to look after them. Does it mean he wants a divorce as well?

SUE No, you get a different bit of paper for a divorce. That's just the kids. We'll have to get a solicitor.

CAROL I'll have to get legal aid.

SARA (*to* SUE *and* CAROL) I got legal aid, and didn't have to pay anything. Some women, even if they don't earn much, often have to pay a proportion of the costs. It also depends on whether they think you have a strong chance of winning your case. I'd rather have had to pay and kept Lisa.

CAROL I thought he'd leave us alone now.

SARA You'd better wear a dress in court.

SUE Get someone to do affadivits for you, you know, saying you're a good mother, that the kids are happy.

ELIZABETH Chris, read this.

CHRIS (*crosses to above* ELIZABETH , *stands*) 'I have known Mrs Grant for two years, since her son Daniel started school, and for this last year I have been his class teacher. He is a very lively and intelligent little boy and as far as I have been able to observe has never shown any undue signs of distress or maladjustment. He is always neatly dressed — ' is she talking about the same kid? — 'and obviously well looked after. I have always found Mrs Grant to be very concerned about her child's welfare and progress.' That's fine.

CHRIS *leaves the stage to operate the slide projector.*

CAROL Nick earns more than the two of us put together.

SUE We earn enough to look after them properly.

CAROL Here, don't they send people round to look at the flat if it's custody.

SUE I've heard about that.

CAROL You don't think they can prove anything about us, do you?

SUE Not unless they put a camera in the bedroom.

CAROL   There ain't enough room for that.

SARA   (*stands, takes her folder*) Regular weekly access by the mother may be reasonably worked out between the two parties.

She sits on chair, up left. The MAN *sits on the chair up right.*

Scene Four

Slides of SUE *and Lennie.*

SUE   Peter and I had joint custody but he had care and control. Lennie lives with him. He and Stella have just had a baby.

Peter didn't bring Lennie to us last weekend because he said he couldn't afford the petrol. Another time he said his windscreen wipers were broken. I never know till the last minute whether Lennie will come or not. Once or twice Lennie's said he doesn't want to go back to his Dad. I don't know what to think. It's like an open wound that won't heal. Sometimes I'm almost relieved when he goes away again. I know it's an awful thing to say, but it's so upsetting.

CAROL   Here, Sue, I hope they don't talk like the forms. I won't understand a word. Do I call him 'Your Lordship', or 'Your Worship'?

Scene Five

CAROL *stands.*

AUTHORITY(MALE *stands*) Mrs Denver, you seem to imply that most people think of children as static. What do you mean by that?

CAROL   It seems to me from the way the questions are being put, that everyone seems to think that children sit quietly in one place all day. See, I know my children. I know what they're thinking. I find that very hard to get across to people who don't have children.

AUTHORITY (MALE)   Are you suggesting that we're all childless here?

CAROL   No. It's just that being a mother, even if I'm not with my children, I'm thinking about them. You see, you're not in contact with my children, that's what I'm trying to say. That I see my children differently from you.

AUTHORITY (MALE)   So you think you have a unique experience of children. Is that what you're trying to say?

CAROL   No. Just with my children.

AUTHORITY (MALE)   But are you suggesting that you have some unique experience over everyone in this court of all children?

CAROL   No. Only my children. (*She sits.* AUTHORITY *sits on chair right*)

———

Scene Six

ELIZABETH *stands.*

AUTHORITY (SUE *stands*) Mrs Grant, your former husband has stated that you did not exert yourself to feed the child or care for his physical needs. What do you say to that?

ELIZABETH   I did feed him and care for his physical needs. I don't think you can do that without exerting yourself. I mean, from my knowledge of children, if you don't look after them, they soon make their presence felt.

AUTHORITY (SUE)   He also states that you were careless and slovenly in your ways and set the child a bad example.

ELIZABETH   It's a matter of degree what one means by 'careless and slovenly'.

AUTHORITY (SUE)   But if, for example, you made yourself a snack in the kitchen, you might leave the food and utensils on the worktop — the loaf, the crumbs, the dirty knife, the butter packet, the lidless jampot and so on.

ELIZABETH   I might well do that sometimes, but I would always clear up afterwards. When you have a child and other commitments, you don't necessarily wash up every plate the minute you use it. Actually, I am very systematic in the kitchen. I treat it as a place of work.

AUTHORITY (SUE)   I believe you said that when friends came for the evening, your husband enjoyed doing the cooking. Is that your evidence?

ELIZABETH   Yes.

AUTHORITY (SUE)   And this was the case with the witness who stayed overnight on several occasions?

ELIZABETH   Yes.

AUTHORITY (SUE)   Tell us what happened on these occasions.

ELIZABETH   Often he would come on Saturday, have dinner with us, and then, because he would stay talking till very late, my husband would offer him the spare bed and he would stay for breakfast.

AUTHORITY (SUE)   Who would make breakfast on these occasions?

GERALD   I did.

AUTHORITY (SUE)   Why didn't she make breakfast?

GERALD   She never thought about it.

ELIZABETH   If my husband was happy to get up and make breakfast, then I was happy to let him.

AUTHORITY (SARA)   'Making breakfast' is nowadays an uncertain phrase, isn't it? It might mean tipping some cornflakes into a plate and putting on the kettle. The idea of six silver entrée dishes with different cooked things inside them is getting a bit obsolete.

AUTHORITY (SUE)   Mrs Grant, I wasn't suggesting that you should get up and formally cook things and put them on a hot plate, but when guests came, wouldn't you regard it as your duty to get up and make breakfast? Your son would have to have breakfast, wouldn't he?

ELIZABETH   As I said, if my husband chose to make breakfast on those occasions, I was happy to let him do so. He would never cook breakfast any other time.

GERALD   Are you seriously suggesting that I put on a special show when guests came?

ELIZABETH   I am saying that, yes, definitely.

GERALD   I see.

AUTHORITY (SUE)   So it comes down to this: that any witness that your husband can call to say that he made breakfast and not you, or that he did the cooking for the evening meal and not you, is merely saying what happened exceptionally, when your husband was putting on a show when visitors were present. Is that your evidence?

ELIZABETH   It is.

SUE *sits, near* CAROL.

———

Scene Seven

CAROL (*to* SUE)   Nick can't even sugar his own tea, let alone look after two kids.

———

Scene Eight

AUTHORITY (SARA *stands*) Your husband did not approve of your involvement in the feminist movement, did he?

ELIZABETH   That is right.

AUTHORITY (SARA) You were aware that your husband believed your involvement in the feminist movement prevented you from carrying out the duties and obligations of a mother?

ELIZABETH   My husband always disapproved of any attempt of mine to do anything outside the house, whether it be work, study, going to meet friends — anything.

AUTHORITY (SARA) In the summer of 1976, you were still very much a committed member of the feminist movement?

ELIZABETH   Committed in my head, but not much of my time was committed because I had very little time to commit. Since the divorce my responsibility to my son has always come first.

SARA *sits*.

AUTHORITY (SUE *stands*) Would you say that you deliberately took a part-time job in order to provoke your husband?

ELIZABETH   No, I wouldn't say that. Our son was about to start play-school and I wanted work that involved and interested me. I also needed the money. (*She goes to sit on box down right*)

Scene Nine

CHRIS *enters and sits on box near* ELIZABETH.

ELIZABETH   What time is it?

CHRIS   About three-thirty.

ELIZABETH   Can you collect Dan from school? (*They talk quietly*)

AUTHORITY (SUE *faces audience*) For the purpose of this case, I would like to suggest that in the friends and associates she found in the Women's Liberation Movement, she found an atmosphere sympathetic to her decision to free herself from what she saw as the shackles of married life. She thus found a philosophy which justified the personal position she had adopted. (*To* ELIZABETH) You said you wanted independence, yet you were married. Are you suggesting that you can be married and independent? (*She sits on box near* CAROL)

———

Scene Ten

AUTHORITY (CHRIS. *crosses to near* CAROL) Do you intend to continue working?

CAROL   Yes. I need to support myself and the kids. My husband never paid me any maintenance.

AUTHORITY (CHRIS)   What arrangements do you make to take your daughter to school in the morning, and collect her?

SUE   I take her to school in the morning, because Mrs Denver starts work at eight-thirty.

CAROL   And I pick her up at three-thirty, when I leave work.

AUTHORITY (CHRIS)   And the younger child, the three-year-old?

CAROL   I work in a nursery, so Alex comes with me.

AUTHORITY (CHRIS)   He attends the same nursery?

CAROL   Yes.

AUTHORITY (CHRIS)   Is there any reason why these arrangements could not continue?

CAROL   No.

SUE   None at all.

———

Scene Eleven

AUTHORITY (SARA *stands*)   What do you mean when you say this application for custody is an attempt to 'push the property'?

ELIZABETH (*stands*)   I think my former husband wants the house.

CAROL   Nick's on the housing list.

AUTHORITY (SARA)   You jointly own the house, is that correct?

ELIZABETH   Yes. But when Gerald left, Dan and I stayed.

CAROL   Mrs Harris and I rent this flat together.

AUTHORITY (SARA)   In your own mind, do you link custody with property?

CAROL   I suppose he thinks if he's got the kids, he'll get a place quicker.

ELIZABETH   Insofar as this has always been Dan's home, yes. But if I had to leave the house for some reason, I would obviously try and find accommodation suitable for a child.

CAROL   I've got me name down for a flat in Brixton.

AUTHORITY (SARA)   You and your husband have not considered selling the house?

CAROL   We've got two bedrooms and a living-room.

AUTHORITY (CHRIS)   Do you and Mrs Harris share this double bed?

SUE   Don't answer that. You're not supposed to answer personal questions.

CHRIS *and* ELIZABETH *sit on box down right;* SARA *sits on chair up left.*

———

Scene Twelve

AUTHORITY (MALE *stands*)   Why did you not tell Mrs Cregan, the welfare officer, that you were a lesbian, when she asked you a direct question?

CAROL (*stands*)   I thought she was just meant to come and see if the children were alright, if the place was clean. I thought everything else they leave for the court to sort out.

AUTHORITY (MALE)   Would you accept that by deciding to adopt a homosexual way of life, you were flying in the face of what took place in the marriage ceremony between you and your husband?

CAROL   It wasn't that I decided to adopt a homosexual way of life. I was trying to find a warm and loving relationship. You see, in the marriage ceremony my husband said he would love and cherish me, and he didn't. (*She sits*)

AUTHORITY (MALE *to audience*)   I would like to point out that there might be other women in similar circumstances who thought they might be justified in leaving their husbands, if they took the romantic view that love would triumph over all, and that there was no danger of them losing their children. It should be brought home to them that there is a grave danger that they will lose their children, if they choose to behave in this way. (*He sits on the chair, upright*)

———

Scene Thirteen

ELIZABETH *stands*.

AUTHORITY (SARA) You accept, do you not, that had you not become involved in the feminist movement, you would not have got divorced?

ELIZABETH No, I don't. The break-up of our marriage, as I see it, stemmed from the way my husband treated me, the lack of support and so on. That is how it ended.

AUTHORITY (SARA) You have already said in evidence that you are a participant in the Women's Lib Movement?

ELIZABETH I participate in the Women's Liberation Movement, yes.

AUTHORITY (SARA) You are correcting me, are you, for using the shortened form?

ELIZABETH Yes.

AUTHORITY (SARA) I will try not to do it again. The Women's Liberation Movement has various forms, has it not? At one end of the scale an extreme form, and at the other end of the scale a moderate form. Would you agree?

ELIZABETH Yes, I would agree with that.

AUTHORITY (SARA) And where would you say your views come in this scale?

ELIZABETH I would say I have been moderate in my views.

AUTHORITY (SARA) That means, does it not, that you approve of and fight for equal opportunities and equal pay for women?

ELIZABETH Yes, it does.

AUTHORITY (SARA) What other views do you have apart from equal opportunities and equal pay for women?

ELIZABETH Well, I've been involved in a number of campaigns. I've been involved in a campaign to get free contraception everywhere on the National Health, and in the campaign for free abortion on demand.

AUTHORITY (SUE *stands*) There are some extreme views, are there not, in the Women's Liberation Movement, that the family unit should be overthrown?

ELIZABETH You could say that, yes.

AUTHORITY (SUE) And a view that marriage is a state of subjection?

ELIZABETH I have heard that, yes.

AUTHORITY (SUE) One extreme view, and I hope I'm using the right phrase, is that marriage is a form of legalised rape?

ELIZABETH Yes, I have seen that written.

AUTHORITY (SUE)   Is abortion tied in with that view? In the sense that it involves killing in effigy, as it were, the man who rapes the woman?

ELIZABETH   That's an extraordinary way of putting it. The idea behind the abortion campaign, as I see it, is that every child should be wanted by its mother.

GERALD   She has expressed the view to me that fathers are unnecessary.

ELIZABETH   No, I haven't said that. I think that happy marriages are a good thing and unhappy marriages a very bad thing. I think that where the family unit cannot work, it is better that the people in it should separate.

AUTHORITY (SUE)   So you would agree with all the views I have just summarised?

ELIZABETH   I would not use the same phrases. But I do believe that a woman should be able to choose whether or not she wishes to be married, and whether or not to have a child, without being financially or in any other way dependent on her husband.

AUTHORITY (SUE)   And how would you describe that in terms of family life?

ELIZABETH   If the family life works, then fine. If it doesn't, people need to develop other, more responsible ways of living together. (SUE *sits*)

AUTHORITY (SARA)   Do you read Women's Liberation literature?

ELIZABETH   I do, yes.

AUTHORITY (SARA)   And you read it because in the main you accept the views put forward in the literature?

ELIZABETH   I suppose so. I read things that interest me. Sometimes I disagree with what I read. But I read all kinds of literature, not just Women's Liberation literature.

AUTHORITY (SARA)   You have had some of this literature in your home? Pamphlets, a magazine called *Shrew*, that sort of thing?

ELIZABETH   Yes.

GERALD (*stands*)   And copies of a magazine called *Spare Rib*.

AUTHORITY (SARA)   I would like to suggest to you that some of the articles in these publications represent your views as you have put them forward to your former husband on several occasions.

ELIZABETH   I daresay some of them do represent my views.

AUTHORITY (SARA)   Would you look at this article, from one of these publications. (*She hands the article to* ELIZABETH)

GERALD   The one called 'Women and Sexuality'.

AUTHORITY (SARA)   Does this article express the sort of views about sexual matters that you expressed to your husband?

ELIZABETH   I am sorry, but this is a very long article and I haven't seen it for some time. It looks to me like a very personal account by someone who is a lesbian. It seems to be very personal, very detailed. I am not sure whether one could say it was expressing a view. I don't know whether I would agree or disagree with any views in it without time to re-read it and think about it.

GERALD   You told me that you wanted to be free to form other sexual relationships.

ELIZABETH   That was one of the things I told him, yes.

GERALD   That's the sort of suggestion made in these magazines, including relationships with other women.

AUTHORITY (SARA)   Is that so?

ELIZABETH   I suppose it is.

GERALD   The article also expresses the view that a woman is entitled to be bisexual and to obtain satisfaction in that way.

AUTHORITY (SARA)   Would you agree with that or would you disagree?

ELIZABETH   I would agree that people are entitled to. I mean, it isn't illegal, is it? I don't know exactly what you expect me to say.

AUTHORITY (SARA)   Some of these magazines have drawings.

GERALD   Diagrams, of a sexual nature.

ELIZABETH   They are informative, yes.

AUTHORITY (SARA)   Would you leave these magazines lying around at home where your son might see them?

ELIZABETH   I usually keep them in my bedroom.

GERALD   Sometimes they are in other rooms.

ELIZABETH   I don't think there is anything in them that would be harmful to my son. (*She sits on the box, down right.* GERALD *and* SARA *sit on the chairs*)

————

Scene Fourteen

AUTHORITY (CHRIS *stands*)   Mrs Denver, do your children ever see you in bed together?

CAROL (*stands*)   Julie often brings us tea and toast on a Sunday morning and we all sit round having breakfast together.

AUTHORITY (CHRIS)   Do you leave any appliances lying around?

CAROL   You what?

AUTHORITY (CHRIS)   Do you have any appliances?

CAROL   Well, we've got an electric toaster, but it's broken, so we use the grill. (*She sits*)

———

Scene Fifteen

AUTHORITY (CHRIS)   How is the sex act between lesbians accomplished?

AUTHORITY (SARA *stands*)   It would vary, depending on the individual couple.

AUTHORITY (CHRIS)   How would you expect it to be accomplished?

AUTHORITY (SARA)   The most common form of sexual expression between two females is by mutual manipulation of the genitalia.

AUTHORITY (CHRIS)   Would you consider that normal?

AUTHORITY (SARA)   Normal in terms of statistics, or psychologically healthy?

AUTHORITY (CHRIS)   I'm not sure what you mean.

AUTHORITY (SARA)   Well, the act itself would be the same if practised by heterosexuals. Oral genitalia sex is practised by some eighty per cent of heterosexuals, so the act itself is the same as that practised by most people. The incidence of acts performed between adults of the same sex, based on Kinsey's data, is one in three, so while it is a minor practice, it is very substantially minor. We are talking about a lot of people.

AUTHORITY (CHRIS)   One in three! (*She sits on box down right,* SARA *sits on chair*)

———

Scene Sixteen

AUTHORITY (SUE *stands*)   So you would say that the movement is very much tied in with lesbianism?

ELIZABETH (*stands*)   No, I would not say that it was very much tied in with lesbianism, but I know that a number of women in the movement are lesbians.

AUTHORITY (SUE)   Would it be right to say that your friends consisted of, or certainly included, divorced women and lesbian women?

ELIZABETH   Yes, it would be right to say that. It would also be right to say that women I have met through my husband included divorced and lesbian women, and women I have met through my work.

GERALD   I would say that her dissatisfaction with our marriage dates from the time she first became involved with the movement.

AUTHORITY (SUE)   Is this so?

ELIZABETH   No. Our marriage was unhappy for some years before that.

GERALD   As she became increasingly involved in the movement, her attitude towards our marriage became more resentful.

AUTHORITY (SUE)   Is this true?

ELIZABETH   I did become more resentful, but not because of the women's movement. Because my marriage deteriorated more rapidly over the last three years.

GERALD   She told me on a number of occasions that she had no interest in a secure marriage, and that it was her view that she should be able to have casual affairs with men and women, like her friends did.

AUTHORITY (SUE)   Have you said this?

ELIZABETH   No. (*She goes to sit near* CHRIS)

Scene Seventeen

AUTHORITY (MALE)   Is it possible for homosexuality to appear later in life?

AUTHORITY (SARA)   Yes, it is quite possible. A substantial number of women do not know they are homosexuals at all until after they have had children. This is true of many women homosexuals. Women often marry and have children without any knowledge of orgasm, for instance. They have simply not been taught about it, or have not discovered it. Then, after they have had children, they may, at the age of thirty or forty, or even older, discover that they are passionately sexually aroused by another woman.

CHRIS *takes* ELIZABETH'*s hand.*

You see, in order to discover that you are homosexual, you need to be sufficiently unafraid of your own sexuality to be able to think of someone else of the same sex.

CHRIS *and* ELIZABETH *kiss gently.*

AUTHORITY (MALE)   In your experience, has this discovery late in life affected their attitude towards motherhood?

AUTHORITY (SARA)   No. Sexual choice doesn't necessarily have anything to do with whether one wants to be a parent, or whether one is a good mother.

AUTHORITY (MALE)   How would you characterise the sexuality of a woman in Mrs Denver's position?

AUTHORITY (SARA)   I do not regard this case as one of homosexuality, but of bisexuality. Since both parties have taken part in homosexual and heterosexual acts, it would give me some concern that neither appears to have elected a final course of sexual orientation. It may be that one or the other will revert to heterosexual tendencies. This affects the stability of the relationship.

———

Scene Eighteen

AUTHORITY (MALE *stands*)   You are in your own mind quite certain that there is nothing morally reprehensible whatsoever about your relationship?

CAROL (*stands*)   I am absolutely certain, yes.

AUTHORITY (MALE)   But would you accept that a homosexual relationship was not very normal?

CAROL   No, I would not accept anything like that.

AUTHORITY (MALE)   They frankly recognise their deviation. (*He sits.* CAROL *returns to box, down left*)

———

Scene Nineteen

SUE, ELIZABETH, CHRIS, SARA *stand.*

AUTHORITY (SUE)   To return to the months before your separation. How regularly did Miss Williams visit your home?

ELIZABETH   I don't know. I didn't count.

AUTHORITY (SARA) Mr Grant claims he discovered you and his wife one evening under compromising circumstances. He said: 'I believe you are a lesbian. I think it is unhealthy for my son. Will you please go?' And you refused. Why did you refuse?

CHRIS Mr Grant was being offensive and threatening. I stayed at Mrs Grant's request.

AUTHORITY (SUE) As Miss Williams seems fairly extreme in her views, perhaps you could try to help us.

ELIZABETH I really can't give you a more accurate answer.

AUTHORITY (SARA) Why did you become a regular visitor to the house?

CHRIS We became good friends. Also, at the time Mr Grant was putting a lot of pressure on her and harassing her and the child. I felt she needed a lot of support.

AUTHORITY (SUE) When she did visit your home, did she stay overnight?

ELIZABETH Occasionally, if she stayed very late.

AUTHORITY (SARA) How did you show this support?

CHRIS All sorts of ways. Being able to talk, discuss things, help her not to feel so lonely and isolated. Moral support, I suppose. I think everyone needs emotional support at some time in their lives.

AUTHORITY (SUE) What sort of meals would she have been given when she stayed on these occasions?

ELIZABETH It would depend. Tea, an evening meal, perhaps.

AUTHORITY (SUE) On the occasion he found Miss Williams in the house, your former husband claims that you harassed him by following him round the room, deliberately knocking into him and bumping against him.

ELIZABETH That is not right.

AUTHORITY (SUE) He says you became hysterical and began butting him with your head. He then grasped you by the hair in order to defend himself.

ELIZABETH He was shouting at me and when I ignored him he grabbed my hair so that he could shout straight into my face. I was sitting with my face averted and this seemed to annoy him more than anything.

AUTHORITY (SUE) Your husband admits he told you to get out and probably get stuffed. 'Get stuffed' — that's a phrase that you and your Women's Liberation friends often use, isn't it?

ELIZABETH No, I don't believe it is.

AUTHORITY (SARA) So you felt that she needed protection from her husband?

CHRIS I did not say protection, I said support.

AUTHORITY (SARA)   Does support sometimes entail protection?

CHRIS   Possibly. But not in this case.

AUTHORITY (SARA)   Can you distinguish between the two?

CHRIS   Protection means to shield from something. Support means to give someone additional courage to make their point.

AUTHORITY (SARA)   So you would not stand in the way of brick-bats coming her way, but would attempt to bolster up her ability to fend them off?

CHRIS   I would support her in any way I could.

AUTHORITY (SUE)   How would you describe your relationship with Miss Williams?

ELIZABETH   I would describe it as a close and continuing friendship. She has got to know Dan very well and this is very important to me.

AUTHORITY (SUE)   Mr Grant feels that this woman is an unhealthy influence on the boy. He is unhappy about a woman who is known to be homosexual spending so much time with his son, taking him to her flat. She obviously resents men.

ELIZABETH *and* CHRIS *sit on box down right;* SUE *sits on box down left;* SARA *sits on chair.*

———

Scene Twenty

CHRIS (*to* ELIZABETH)   We were taken into this little room by these psychiatrists.

AUTHORITY (SARA)   She had brought some photographs with her. The boy took the photographs and sat near me describing the photographs and identifying the people in them. He pointed to a nude picture of himself and said: 'That's my sausage, isn't it?' Then he said: 'Cut it off with a scissors.'

CHRIS   He never said that. I was in the room and he never said that.

ELIZABETH   Anyway, that picture was of Alice's little boy. Dan never calls his penis a sausage. He knows what it's called.

CHRIS   I asked him afterwards and he said: 'That's silly, it isn't a sausage.'

AUTHORITY (SARA)   I did not regard Miss Williams as a reliable witness whose evidence I could trust. She is altogether too much identified with the mother's interests.

AUTHORITY (SUE)   Would you say that the mother's friendship with Miss Williams is having an adverse effect on the child?

AUTHORITY (SARA)   During the period of one hour that I spent with the boy, I found him obsessively playing with cars, crashing them into each other. This, I would say, indicated a preoccupation with sexual intercourse. He was constantly calling for a repair service. I would interpret this as a call for help.

AUTHORITY (MALE)   How would you see his prospects for the future?

AUTHORITY (SARA)   At the moment he is a healthy, aggressive little boy. I think, however, that he would be bound to suffer great anxiety over his masculinity, both sexually and non-sexually. He would no doubt feel he had to compensate by taking up a passive, non-aggressive role, a woman's role.

———

Scene Twenty-One

AUTHORITY (MALE *stands*)   In what direction would you encourage your children's sexual orientation?

CAROL (*stands*)   I don't know if you can. I suppose it would be easier if they were heterosexual, but it's up to them. I wouldn't push them one way or the other.

AUTHORITY (MALE)   So it's alright for you to be homosexual but not for them?

CAROL   If I encourage them to be homosexual I'm wrong, if I encourage them to be heterosexual I'm wrong.

AUTHORITY (SARA)   There are a number of factors in this case which cause me great concern. How, for example, will the children know the difference between this surrogate female father-figure and a real male? What are the chances that the lover will molest the daughter?

AUTHORITY (MALE)   Tell me, how do the children deal with the fact that they are living in a homosexual household? Have you, for example, ever felt it necessary to explain to them what part Mrs Harris plays in your life?

CAROL   Not in so many words. They know she loves them and they know our life together is happy. Or are you dwelling again on the sexual aspect?

AUTHORITY (MALE)   I do not wish to dwell on it, but it is an important aspect, is it not?

CAROL   It does seem to be, yes.

———

Scene Twenty-Two

> *The cast leave the stage, except for* SARA *and the* MAN.

AUTHORITY (SARA *stands centre stage*)   Judgement in the case of Grant versus Grant.

> This has been a difficult case, not least because we have had laid bare to us the gradual and painful erosion of a secure family unit. It is up to the court to decide what the cause of this breakdown was, and to judge the custody case accordingly.

> It could be suggested that the mother's personal opinions about family life, exemplified by her passionate interests in the Women's Liberation Movement, are likely to have a damaging effect upon her young son. If he is brought up by her, she will teach him to have little or no respect for the ordinary obligations of family life. He is also likely to be taught doctrines about sexual morality which could be extremely dangerous and expose him to unnecessary risks in adolescence. If he continues to live with his mother, he is likely to live in a hothouse atmosphere of feminist fanaticism, which is very far from the ordinary balance of life of other children.

> Where the evidence of Mrs Grant conflicted with that of Mr Grant, save in some quite minor details, I was confident that the father gave me a reasonably objective account of the development of the family relations, and the mother did not. I am afraid I find that she was not at all candid on a number of matters.

> The mother appears to have developed an increasing resentment of the father, and of men in general. She has reached the stage where no man can do anything right, and regards herself as caught up in a man-made world. I would remind you of my question to her: 'Is your attitude to law still that it is a man-made bureaucracy?' And her reply: 'Yes, it is certainly patriarchal. There are only, I think, two or three women judges.'

> In view of her views, it is not surprising that her husband should, in the closing stages of the marriage, have been provoked to some violence. The truth is that she decided to organise her life in such a way as to throw upon her husband more and more of the housekeeping. He cut up rough in the end, and he was pretty rough, but she brought it all on herself.

> In view, therefore, of his intention to remarry, and his eagerness provide the child with a secure and normal family life, we award custody t the natural father.

She leaves the stage.

———

Scene Twenty-Three

AUTHORITY (MALE *stands centre stage*) Judgement in the case of Denver versus Denver.

I would like to remind everyone present here that ten years ago this case would have been disposed of very quickly indeed once the defendant had been shown to be a homosexual.

But things have moved rather rapidly in the past decade, and we have been deeply concerned to approach this case with as open a mind as possible. As we all know, divorce is much easier today than it has ever been in our society. But this should not leave us callous of the interests of the innocent children of these broken marriages. It is their best interests we must keep in mind.

Clearly we must face the dangers: a boy and a girl growing up without a strong father-figure in the home. Also the dangers of gossip. However, there are other, balancing factors which must be considered.

Firstly, it is clear that neither Mrs Denver nor her lover consider their relationship to be disreputable, indecent or offensive and they have both at all times cared well for the children. Secondly, from the evidence I have heard of the father's circumstances, he has not offered, to my mind, any suitable alternative arrangements for the day-to-day care of the children. He has no immediate plans for remarriage — indeed, so far he has not even considered divorce proceedings.

Therefore, in the absence of a surrogate mother, I grant custody, care and control to the natural mother; under the following conditions: that the lesbian couple keep their relationship as private as possible, and do not display their affection too explicitly in front of the children. I suggest they occupy separate rooms from now on.

I hope no one will regard this as containing any judgement for or against homosexual parents. The fact of their lesbianism in no way affects the judgement on the custody of the children. In this case the father simply could not offer physically adequate care which could replace that of the natural mother.

The verdict rests on the narrow grounds of bricks and mortar and nothing else. (*He exits*)

Pulse music: 'Inception'. Slides: CAROL *and her kids;* SUE *alone;* ELIZABETH *alone;* SARA *alone.*

THE END

MY MOTHER SAYS I NEVER SHOULD
Women's Theatre Group

My Mother Says I Never Should was written in the autumn of 1974. It was our first play produced specifically for a section of the non-theatre-going public, in this case teenagers. Our aim was to perform for them in their own places of work and entertainment, i.e. schools and youth clubs.

We decided that we wanted to examine the contradictory situation experienced by adolescent girls and expose the double standard implicit in people's responses to the sexual behaviour of boys and girls. We set out to create a play which would lead to discussion about contraception and abortion. Existing literature on the subject for teenagers was sparse and moralistic: it carried warnings about promiscuity and VD, contained assumptions about the 'natural' differences between the sexuality of boys and girls, and stressed that the best answer for girls to give was always 'no'. Although we wanted to challenge such moral imperatives, we also felt it important to show our respect for the fact that some people didn't feel like having sex whether it was prohibited or not. But, on balance, given the conservative nature of most advice both at home and at school, we felt it essential to present without disapproval an example of a girl who wasn't going steady and who said 'yes' because she wanted to. We made her fifteen because we also wanted to question the legal anomaly which makes the age of consent sixteen and assumes that teenagers are too young to have sex because they are too young to have children. Our objective was to provide information and encourage girls to see themselves as active agents capable of making real choices in their lives.

Having decided on the general issues that we wanted to raise, we did a lot of research: we talked to girls, teachers and parents (and were amazed at the levels of fear, prejudice and ignorance), we studied contraceptive techniques and the dissemination of advice to young people. Then we pooled our information, created characters and a plot, improvised, and finally went off in twos and threes to write and rewrite. Writing was a long and often painful business, inevitably there were disagreements and compromises, but we also gave each other confidence and took greater risks. Ultimately we felt that the group process distilled a clarity not obtainable by us individually. The way in which we wrote was affected both by the content of the play and the proposed audience; there was a wariness of experimental 'artistic' theatre as well as of stark agitprop forms, because we felt that the most effective way of making sense to an audience whose principal theatrical experience had been mediated by television, was to use a conventional TV style with a story and lots of laughs.

Our method of conveying new ideas was to create characters whom the audience could recognise and identify with, then show how these characters learn to understand and change their personal situations. Because of the importance of this identification process we paid meticulous attention to styles of dress and speech. And it paid off: probably the most consistent response we had in over one hundred performances was amazement that the two women who played Terri and Wendy were twenty-six and twenty-eight and not fifteen. There are however contradictions in trying to engage our audience through this type of identification: there is always the danger that attitudes which are presented in order to be criticised can actually be reinforced by being re-experienced in the context of the play — for example the girls' tremendous concern with their appearance could be construed as behaviour we found acceptable. Possibilities for this kind of mis-interpretation were minimised because of the discussions which took place after the play and which formed an integral part of each performance.

When the acting was over, we would change into our normal clothes and with members of the audience, in small groups or all together, we would examine the issues which had been raised. Sometimes, particularly in schools, this took the form of improvisation: we would propose, for example, that a girl imagine that she was pregnant and that she had to tell her parents. The success of the discussions depended to a great extent on our involvement in all aspects of the production: we had to know about methods of contraception as well as to be able to defend the arguments the play presented. In response to points made by our audience, we continued to make changes in the text where we felt it necessary.

The way in which we initially gained access to this new audience of teenagers was by performing for two weeks at the Oval House Theatre Club, and inviting the ILEA Drama Inspector and educational journalists as well as the usual critics. From this we established a network of contacts through which we eventually obtained one or two bookings every day. (By then our work was subsidised by the Arts Council and GLAA.) We performed in schools, youth clubs, colleges of education, universities, women's centres, political meetings, and benefits. Occasionally we encountered intense opposition: one teacher walked out with his whole class in the middle of a performance; at a youth club the performance was sabotaged by boys swinging Tarzan-fashion from ropes. Performances were cancelled when Head Teachers discovered the content of our play and our style of discussion. There were criticisms from within the Women's Movement at our recommendation of the pill. But mostly the play really worked; kids stayed on after home-time to talk to us and help load the van. 'I just never saw things in that way before' was a typical comment. Sometimes hysterical laughter covered a sense of shock and delight that we as adults should be presenting forbidden topics. One youth worker told us that after our play girls had come to her for the first time with questions and problems, and that they continued to talk about the play for months afterwards. A group of boys at a National Union of School Students conference talked about the lack of guidelines for non-sexist behaviour. The play was an important event for a lot of young people. And the ILEA Health inspector also seemed to like it: 'Excellent, really excellent. Covered all the issues. I wonder if your next play could be about teeth.'

We stopped performing *My Mother Says I Never Should* at the end of 1975. In 1976 the Inner London Education Authority Television Centre made a video-tape of it as a teaching resource for schools. It was used extensively and copies are still available, but in 1978 transmissions from ILEA were stopped — in response to complaints made by staff and parents. In spite of the apparent liberalisation of public opinion, the issues raised in the play continued to be contentious. In December 1978 the *Evening Standard* published a four column letter from a London teacher, headlined 'Incitement to Sex In a Film for Schools'. In it the teacher suggests that the disproportionate number of pregnancies among London schoolgirls could be attributed to the fact that 'thousands of children in ILEA schools have been shown a propaganda film encouraging them to go to the Brook Centres for contraceptives'. The astonishing letter goes on to quote sections of the play and concludes that, '*My Mother Says I Never Should* actually incites under-age children to have sexual intercourse and break the law.' The writer is of course referring not to children but to *girls*. The struggle for women to gain autonomy and control over their sexuality and fertility will be a long one.

Mica Nava

My Mother Says I Never Should was first performed in early 1975 at Oval House, London.

CAST

SINGER
BABY GIRL
BABY BOY
DIANE, hairdresser, about 22
TERRI and WENDY, school friends, about 15
GRAN, Terri's grandmother
SHEILA, Terri's mother
TEACHER at Terri and Wendy's school
DOCTOR at the family planning clinic

The BABY GIRL and SHEILA were played by the same person; the BABY BOY and the TEACHER were played by the same person; GRAN and the DOCTOR were played by the same person. The songs can be divided between the performers.

The play was devised, written, performed and directed by the Women's Theatre Group, which at the time consisted of Frankie Armstrong, Lyn Ashley, Clair Chapman, Sue Eatwell, Anne Engel, Jane Meadows, Mica Nava.

ACT ONE

The set in the original touring production consisted of two canvas bookflats, linked by a hospital-type screen on wheels; this arrangement separated off a back-stage area where costume changes and sound control took place, and enabled the group to perform in places like youth clubs which had no special performing facilities. The basic set on stage consisted of a table (2' × 3') three chairs, and a stool for the singer. There were no special lighting effects (although on the rare occasions where facilities existed, lights would not be brought up until the entrance of the babies). Music, voice-overs and aeroplane noises were pre-recorded on tape and played back. Although good sound equipment is desirable, a simple cassette recorder with sufficient volume would probably be adequate.

Prologue

SINGER   My Mother says I never should
                Play with the boys down in the wood
                If I did, she would say, you'll
                Get yourself in the family way.
                Was she right?
                Was my Mamma right?
                Pity for me if she was right.

Scene One

On tape: sound of church bells followed by aeroplane landing, then airport type announcement.

ANNOUNCER   The 7:15 stork from New York has now arrived. The 7:15 stork from New York has arrived. Would the Carson Twins please report to the reception area. Carson Twins to the reception area, please.

Enter the CARSON TWINS. *They are babies dressed in nappies, bootees, etc. The* GIRL *in pink, trailing a doll; she is bouncy and assertive. The* BOY *is dressed in blue and carrying a gun; has his thumb in his mouth and is sleepy.*

GIRL (*bouncing on*) Here we are at last — The World!!!!

BOY (*with thumb in mouth*) The world.

GIRL   Gee, isn't it exciting?

BOY   Yeah, sure is exciting.

GIRL   Wow, what a journey, eh?????

BOY   Yeah, really was rough.

GIRL   Still, good to be here!!!!

BOY   Yeah, great to be here.

GIRL   Where?

BOY   Where?

GIRL   Yeah, where are we?

BOY   And where are we going!!!!

GIRL *looks at him in mock horror and groans.* BOY *echoes her groan, while a singer sings:*

SINGER   What are little girls made of
         What are little girls made of
         Sugar and spice and all things nice
         That's what little girls are made of.

         What are little boys made of
         What are little boys made of
         Frogs and snails and puppy dogs' tails
         That's what little boys are made of.

The GIRL *spots the gun; dropping her doll she takes it from the* BOY *and investigates it till she makes it work. The* BOY *meanwhile picks up the doll, drops to his knees and cradles it to the end of song. Suddenly a deep authoritative male* VOICE *over loudspeaker system.*

VOICE   I've got a son. A pal to take to the football match. Someone to carry on the family name. A new head of the family. Hey, you; you down there in the blue . . . .

BOY (*clutching on to his sister, frightened*) Who, me.

VOICE   Yes, you. I'm going to make a MAN of you, MY SON.

GIRL (*after a pause*) Hey, what about me, in the pink?

VOICE   My little Princess. Daddy's angel. Take back the doll. (*She does so. In a firmer voice*) Pick up the gun, son, and come with me. (*The* BOY *goes. Sugary voice again*) Oh, and little angel — go and help Mummy in the kitchen, will you? (*The* GIRL *stomps off, cross*)

———

Scene Two

DIANE's *flat.* DIANE *enters with some smart clothes and shoes. She sets these, sits down upstage left and starts to paint her nails. She is fashionably dressed and confident.* TERRI *and* WENDY, *who have been sitting in the front row of the audience, now step onto the stage. The seats are kept free for them throughout the play.*

TERRI (*to the audience*) Hello, I'm Terri, I'm fifteen. I live with me Mum, me Dad and me Gran, oh yes and my brother Jim, who's fourteen, at Swallow House on Maybury Estate. This is my best friend, Wendy.

WENDY I'm two months older than Terri. I can't stand school. I like to enjoy myself. My mum was the same when she was young. We get on smashing, Mum and me; she doesn't bother me, I can do what I like. My dad, he's usually away.

TERRI We both work Saturday mornings at Mr Raymond's, shampooing; and Diane's hairdresser there. (*Indicating* DIANE) We're going round to her flat now so we can play records loud and try on her clothes.

———

Scene Three

The girls walk round to U.S.L. and enter DIANE's *flat. There is loud pop music (the latest hit). The girls greet each other and there is a lot of excitement and giggling as* WENDY *and* TERRI *try on* DIANE's *clothes.*

DIANE You don't half look sexy.

TERRI (*examining herself in an imagined mirror*) I look like a blooming maypole.

WENDY You'll have to fill out a bit more on top before you can carry that off.

DIANE It's how fellas like you that matters, isn't it?

TERRI I'm not bothered about that. Let them think what they like.

WENDY Oh, doesn't this make you feel elegant! (*Draping a silk shawl or similar around her shoulders*)

TERRI You look like a bloody ostrich.

DIANE Brian don't like me in flash things. I haven't worn that since I bought it.

WENDY Oooh, can I borrow it for the party next weekend?

DIANE All right, if you look after it.

WENDY   I asked me mum yesterday night and she said yes . . . What about you, Terri?

TERRI (*trying on shoes*)   I don't know how you go about it. I can never get me mum on her own. Yesterday I was just getting round to it and me dad walks in wanting his tea. I've never stopped out all night and what with it being out of London, I don't think I've got much of a chance.

WENDY   Tell your mum it's Linda. I mean, she is eighteen. You don't have to tell her her mum and dad won't be there.

TERRI   I don't like lying to her . . . she's bound to find out . . . I'll have a go anyway.

WENDY   Well, I'm not going on me own.

DIANE   You going to get your hair done before you go?

WENDY   I'll have to do something to it. Oh Christ, I hope I don't come out in spots. (*Looking in the mirror*) Last week I put banana and avocado all over me face and back, just like it said in *Petticoat*, but it didn't do no good though.

TERRI   You believe everything you read, don't you? Do you know last year she tried sunbathing through a sieve to get freckles. I think it's stupid everyone trying to look the same.

WENDY   Yes, but people look at you all funny if you're not wearing the right things, and no fella would want to be seen with you.

DIANE   Yes, she's right you know; look at you, love, always in trousers. Men don't like that.

TERRI   I wear skirts sometimes. I got a halter neck dress I could wear to the party, but it's short, me legs are all hairy.

DIANE   Don't you shave them, then?

TERRI   No, you've got to keep doing it once you start.

DIANE   It's no different to doing under your arms.

TERRI   I can't be bothered with all that.

WENDY   The trouble with halter necks, you've got to wear a special bra, too.

TERRI   I could try not wearing one, but I'm so small it wouldn't even show.

DIANE   My Brian likes women flopping about.

WENDY   He's a bloody sex maniac, your Brian is.

TERRI   You can talk, I know what's going through your mind when Kevin's about . . .

DIANE   You going to invite him to the party, then?

WENDY   I would if I dared — but he'd think I was easy.

TERRI I think you should. If you want him to go, there's no other way, is there? At least he won't have any trouble with his parents; fellas never do.

DIANE How old is he?

WENDY He's sixteen — but he looks much older.

DIANE Go on, why don't you? I think it's quite a laugh asking them once in a while.

WENDY What if he says no?

TERRI Well, fellas have to risk that, too.

WENDY Do you really think I should?

TERRI *and* DIANE Yes.

WENDY I got his number off his sister, because I arranged to ring her about a cookery class . . .

TERRI You sly cow. (*Hands* WENDY *phone D.S.R.*) Go on then . . .

WENDY (*spotting open* 'Fabulous' *or* 'Petticoat' *on the table*) Ooh, look at my stars; it says 'This weekend your man appeal is at its height,' (*Giggles from* TERRI *and* DIANE. WENDY *takes the phone*) He's never in. (*She dials nervously*) Oh, Hello, Mrs Adams? Is Kevin there . . . (*To* TERRI) Ooh, she's gone to get him. (*Lots of giggling*) Hello, Kevin . . . what? No — it's me, Wendy. Look, my cousin Linda's having a party next weekend in Letchmore Green and she wants some more fellas and Terri thought you might like to go . . .

TERRI Ooh, I never . . .

WENDY Ooh, lovely; see you at the club on Friday then.

TERRI You cow, it's nothing to do with me.

DIANE You didn't dare tell him it was staying the night, did you?

WENDY Oh come on, Terri . . . You've got to come now. Shall I come with you to ask your mum?

TERRI No, that wouldn't do no good. I'll talk to her tonight. If they let me go, can I bring my dress round to show you? Oh no, I'll wear me trousers, I'll feel more comfortable.

WENDY Oh, Terri . . .

DIANE Who are you inviting then?

TERRI I haven't got anyone special. I'm just going to have a good time. What I really like is the dancing.

DIANE We all know where that leads . . .

TERRI That's all you bloody think of . . . I'm not letting anyone bully me.

DIANE   It's not bullying, sometimes you fancy it as much as he does . . . sometimes you fancy it when he don't . . . (*There is a heavy pause*)

TERRI   Umm, if they let me, can we come back here on Saturday and get ready; I don't want me mum fussing about me . . .

DIANE   Yes, of course . . . I'll get Brian to give you a last looking over.

TERRI *and* WENDY   Thanks, 'bye then.

DIANE   If you can't be good, be careful. (DIANE *and* WENDY *leave.* TERRI *moves forward*)

TERRI   If my mum went to parties more like Wendy's mum, she might understand me and let me go. It's not fair . . . (*She sings to the tune of 'My Old Man's a Dustman'*)

My old Mum's a housewife, spends twenty-four hours on call
She works an eighty-hour week and don't get paid at all.
My mate's Mum goes out to work, she works out down the school
And even though she's out all day, the housework's her job too
That's like you've got two bosses, it don't seem very fair
All that cooking, cleaning, washing; Dads should do their share
I'd like to be a doctor, a printer or a chef but everyone you try to tell
You think they'd all gone deaf
If I could get a decent job with decent pay as well
Then I could do the kinds of things I wanted for meself.

———

Scene Four

Later that day. TERRI'*s home. Enter* GRAN *and* MUM (SHEILA), GRAN *with knitting.* MUM *with darning.* GRAN *sits in chair left,* MUM *picks one up from D.S.R. and moves to beside* GRAN.

MUM   Aah, it's nice to get your feet up for a change.

GRAN   I saw that fat old bag Mrs Brown today. She crossed over the road when she seen me coming; dreadful old gossip.

MUM   I'm so tired these days, there's always so much to do. I'd like to get out for a bit, get a part-time job . . .

GRAN   Go on, there's not much to do these days, what with the kids so big . . .

MUM   Be nice to have a bit of money of me own without always having to ask him for it.

GRAN   She stuck her tongue out at the milkman; she must be looney.

MUM   They had an ad. up in the cake shop saying they needed someone, nice
to have a bit of company.

GRAN   Go on, why don't you, then?

MUM   You know Eddie wouldn't let me.

GRAN   I don't know why you pay so much attention to that man, my girl.

TERRI *enters*.

TERRI   Hello Mum, hello Gran . . .

MUM   Hello, love, how was the job today? You hungry? . . .

TERRI   We went round Diane's to play some records; I'm not really hungry.

TERRI   } Mum, Wendy's cousin's havin' a party.
GRAN   } Put the kettle on, love, get your old Gran a cup of tea . . .

MUM   Let her catch her breath, Gran.

TERRI   Can I go, Mum?

MUM   (*looking at darning*)   Now that's not right . . .

TERRI   Can I go!!

MUM   Where, love?

TERRI (*shouting*)   Why don't you listen!

MUM   Don't shout, Terri. (*Shouting*) We can all hear you. Now start again.

TERRI   Can I go to Wendy's cousin's party?

MUM   I should think so, love, 'long as it's on a weekend.

TERRI   And we'd be staying the night, because it's out at Letchmore Green
and it would be too late to come back.

GRAN   What about some tea, Terri?

TERRI (*impatiently*)   Oh Gran . . . well, Mum?

MUM   No love, not for the night.

TERRI   Why not, all the others are?

MUM   What others?

TERRI   Wendy and that — her mum's letting her.

MUM   The less said about Wendy's mum the better.

TERRI   Ooh, Mum . . . (*Mutters*) Here we go again.

MUM   Besides, what would your Dad say?

TERRI   If you told Dad I was at Wendy's he wouldn't worry at all.

GRAN   Look, why don't we talk about it over a nice cup of tea?

MUM   Why don't you make the tea instead of just sitting there — and I'm not
lying to your Dad.

GRAN   He lies to you, you fool.

MUM   That's no excuse.

TERRI   Mum, please, I'm fifteen now, I'm not a baby any more.

MUM   That's just what I'm worried about, my girl.

TERRI   What do you mean?

MUM   Oh — I don't know, Terri — boys and girls, all-night parties . . .

TERRI   It's not an all-night party.

MUM   But you'd be stopping all night!

TERRI   Just sleeping, we've got to take sleeping bags and that. Mum, don't you trust me?

MUM   Oh, I don't know, love, what would people think?

TERRI   What people?

MUM   You've got to think about your reputation now.

TERRI   Oh don't be so old-fashioned. That's stupid.

GRAN   Yes, don't be old-fashioned, Sheila, let her go.

TERRI   Anyway, you let Jim stay out all night and he's younger than me.

MUM   It's different for boys, Terri.

TERRI   Why, no it's not, it's not fair.

MUM   Nobody wants to marry a girl with a reputation.

TERRI   I don't want to get married, I want to go to a party. Anyway, don't boys get a reputation?

MUM   Boys don't fall pregnant, young lady.

TERRI   Mum, I'm not going to do anything like that.

MUM   You never can tell, boys get drinking at a party, and what with the soft lights and the music, and some young man telling you how lovely you are — before you know where you are — you've ruined your life.

TERRI   Oh Mum . . .

GRAN   (*pointedly*)   Terri's not like you, Sheila.

MUM   (*turning on her*)   Stop interfering, Gran. Go and get us some tea, Terri.

TERRI   You know I'm sensible, Mum.

MUM   Go and make the tea, I'll think about it. (TERRI *goes*)

GRAN   Things have changed, Sheila, things are different nowadays. Terri's a sensible young woman, *she* won't be swayed by a pretty word.

MUM   I know she's sensible, but she's so young; it's somebody taking advantage of her I'm worried about, I don't want her to get hurt.

GRAN   Not all men are like your Ed . . .

MUM　He married me, didn't he?

GRAN　Much good it did you, look at you now; you used to be so lovely. Only thirty-five and behaving like an old woman, always tired and moaning; you should leave that man, Sheila.

MUM　And you'd be in a fine pickle if I did. Where would you go, where would I go and what about the kids?

GRAN　You could get a job, the kids'll be earning their own living soon enough.

MUM　I'm too old to start again. What's the point?

GRAN　You'd be leading your own life. That man treats you like a slave. (*Chuckles*) That plumber what came here the other day, I could tell he really fancied you; you took a bit of care of yourself, maybe there'd be others, and then you wouldn't be so mean about Terri.

MUM　Oh, Gran!

TERRI *enters.*

GRAN　Ah, tea, and about time too.

MUM　(*taking tea*) Thanks, love.

TERRI　(*after a pause*) Well, Mum . . .

MUM　Oh I don't know, love, your Gran thinks I should let you go.

TERRI　Oh Gran, thanks. (*Leaps about*)

GRAN　That's right, love. I think you've got your head screwed on right, but you should see about them tablets they have — no point in taking risks.

MUM　What tablets!!!

TERRI　(*spluttering*) Do you mean the Pill, Gran?

GRAN　That's right, for stopping babies, so you can enjoy yourself.

MUM　Gran!!!

GRAN　Just because you don't enjoy it.

MUM　You wicked old woman. I've brought my Terri up to be a good girl and keep herself for the man she marries and you go putting ideas in her head. My Terri doesn't want to go sleeping with men. She's fifteen!

GRAN　I liked it when I was fifteen.

TERRI　Gran, you never . . .

GRAN　It's only natural, isn't it?

TERRI　Well Mum I don't feel like it yet.

MUM　Don't you, love?

TERRI　No, so you needn't worry.

MUM   Well, that's a relief then.

TERRI   Can I go then?

MUM   Where, love?

TERRI   Mum! To Wendy's cousin's party!!

MUM   Ooh, I suppose so, love, but you be careful now . . .

TERRI   Thanks, Mum. Come on, Gran, we'll get the spuds peeled . . . (*They exit*)

SINGER   I've often heard it said, and it's true, I'm sure
There's one law for the rich and another for the poor
But the same thing seems to hold when it comes to me and Jim
It's not Okay for me, but it's quite alright for him.

What's it all about, won't somebody tell us
Why there's one law for us and another for the fellas.

If you're a fella, you can stay out late at night
Get into aggro and come home 'alf tight
Chase the birds, be as randy as you can
And they'll say, 'Ain't it nice 'ow he takes after his old man!'

What's it all about . . . etc.

But if you're a girl, it's a different story
For they say your reputation is your crowning glory
Don't step out of line, though it's dull as hell
Stay pure and demure till you hear those wedding bells.

What's it all about . . . etc.

———

Scene Five

The bathroom at the party the following weekend. TERRI *enters followed by the sound of party music and laughing from offstage. She does her hair and touches up her make-up in front of the mirror. Party sounds again as* WENDY *enters. Both girls are dressed for the occasion.*

TERRI   Bloody hell, where have you been? You left me stuck with that bloke.

WENDY   What bloke?

TERRI   You know, Kevin's friend, the one without a chin. I got lumbered with him, his breath smelt like old socks. Where were you?

WENDY   Do I look funny?

TERRI   Yes, you look as though you've had a bit.

WENDY   Oh don't say that, does it show?

TERRI   Well, I saw you and Kev boozing away on the stairs, he wasn't half having a good feel!

WENDY   I remember, you tripped over us.

TERRI   Didn't think you noticed. Where were you then?

WENDY   Linda's bedroom.

TERRI   . . . You haven't!!

WENDY   I have.

TERRI   What, all the way with Kevin?

WENDY   Yes, well, he wanted to — and he was ever so nice to me . . .

TERRI   I bet he was!

Pause.

How did you manage then?

WENDY   What do you mean, how did I manage? I didn't have to do very much, did I.

TERRI   Oh . . . Did he take your clothes off?

WENDY   Well, bits.

TERRI   Did he take everything off?

WENDY   How do I know, the light was off. Anyway there were coats all over the place — I couldn't look, could I, that would have been embarrassing . . . Ooh, I must go to the loo. (*Goes behind the screen*)

TERRI (*loudly*)   What was it like? (*Silence*) What was it like, then?

WENDY (*off stage*)   I don't half feel giddy.

TERRI   Did it hurt?

WENDY (*off stage*)   No.

TERRI   Well, go on, was it nice?

WENDY (*off stage*)   Yes . . . it's funny . . . it's quite quick really, you haven't got time to think about it — he said he liked it.

TERRI   Do you feel different now?

WENDY (*re-emerges*)   A bit shook up . . . I felt like crying . . . Do I look different?

TERRI   No, just the same — only drunk. You're not going to get engaged, are you?

WENDY   I don't know.

TERRI   No one saw you, did they?

WENDY   Yes, someone walked in, right in the middle and put the light on, I don't know who it was though. I hope it wasn't Linda.

TERRI   She wouldn't say nothing.

WENDY   My dad thinks she's a nice girl; she's always saying how she's saving herself for Bill when they get married.

TERRI   Don't make no difference. Unless you get pregnant.

WENDY   Ooh — you can't get pregnant the first time!

TERRI   You'd believe anything!!

WENDY   He was saying lovely things to me, and he promised not to let on to his mates, he said he wouldn't.

TERRI   Look, it's no skin off his nose. It's just another feather in his cap. It's you they're gonna talk about.

WENDY   Ooh don't! I must get back . . .

TERRI   What, you going to do it again?

WENDY   Not just yet . . . you come with me and find him, I feel a bit embarrassed.

TERRI   I won't know where to look. (*Both giggle*)

WENDY   Come on. (*They return to their seats in the audience*)

———

Scene Six

WENDY *and* TERRI *are still in their seats in the audience. They have put on school sweaters over their party clothes. Enter* TEACHER, *rather severe and nervous. She hangs up a large diagram of the male and female reproductive organs. She addresses the audience. The lesson is frequently interrupted by* WENDY *and* TERRI's *comments and the rustling of crisp packets, etc.* WENDY *and* TERRI *try and involve the audience.*

TEACHER   Good morning, boys and girls! Nice to see so many of you here. Today we'll be studying human reproduction, and just to refresh your memories, we'll do a quick history of reproductive systems. Now. You'll all remember fission. And if you'll turn to page 132 you'll see an illustration of fission. See? That's fission, right there, the cell divides right in two, just as though you took a sausage in your hands and broke it into two identical parts. Now, fission is what we call asexual reproduction.

WENDY (*aside*)   How boring!

TEACHER   Human beings reproduce sexually, as we say. If you turn to page 232 you'll see two diagrams, one of the male reproductive parts — (*She bashes the diagram of the female parts with her pointer*) — and one of the female reproductive parts — (*She bashes the male parts with her pointer*) — for as we all know, in sexual reproduction, two separate bodies are required, and two totally different types of reproductive organs.

TERRI (*imitating church organ*)   Tum tum te tum!

TEACHER   Now you'll remember the terms 'egg' and 'sperm' from our study of fish. These are also the terms used for human beings. The human egg is tiny, smaller than the head of a pin, but the human sperm is much, much smaller than that. The human egg is twenty thousand times bigger than the human sperm!

WENDY   Is this for the exam, Miss?

TEACHER (*angry*)   Now this is what happens, if you'll all listen carefully; this is what human reproduction is all about: the egg in the female is released from the ovaries, the sperm is ejaculated out of the penis into the vagina where it fertilises the egg, which implants itself in the wall of the uterus and begins to grow. This tiny, fertilised egg contains all the characteristics of the forthcoming infant: dark or fair, blue eyed or brown, dimpled or freckled.

TERRI   Or spotty!

TEACHER   Now the woman's body begins to prepare itself for the coming child. Her body changes in shape and the hormonal balance shifts to accommodate its tiny passenger.

TERRI (*imitates train*)   Whoooo - ooooooooooo!

TEACHER   Within her womb a minute human being grows, developing eyes and feet and fingers.

TERRI   And spots.

TEACHER   This tiny embryo contains all the characteristics of both parents . . . (*A bell rings.* WENDY *and* TERRI *go on to the stage in order to exit*) Girls! Girls! Homework for Monday, diagrams page 232, copy. I'll collect them. (*She begins to roll up the diagram*)

WENDY (*catches* TERRI)   Hey, Terri — wait — you know what she's been going on about . . .

TERRI   Yes.

WENDY   Well, I'm late — I'm nearly three weeks late.

TERRI   Didn't he use nothing?

WENDY   I don't know; it was dark. (WENDY *and* TERRI *exit*)

TEACHER (*to the audience*) Well, what am I supposed to say? This is a biology class, not a — a blue movie, what am I to do, sit there and tell them about sex, just like that? That's their mothers' job.

And they're just babies; some of them just turned fifteen. It's unhealthy of them to have that kind of knowledge at their age.

What could I tell them, anyway — there aren't the words — I'd like to be able to tell them what they want to know about sex, I — just wouldn't know where to begin. (*She exits*)

SINGER   It's so hard for me to tell them
It's so hard to find a way
Why can't I ever find the words to say
What I mean to say . . .

———————

Scene Seven

MUM *enters, tired, collects the ironing board, iron and ironing, moves to centre and starts to iron.*

TERRI   Don't half smell nice. Are we having apple crumble?

MUM   You wait and see . . . you got any homework?

TERRI   No, not really.

MUM   What do you mean, not really?

TERRI   Oh, just biology . . . diagrams and things.

MUM   What sort of diagrams?

TERRI   Humans, insides.

MUM   Ugh, that don't sound very nice.

TERRI   No, it's interesting, but I'm a bit muddled about it, she goes so quick and she only tells us half of it . . .

MUM   The teacher?

TERRI   She's Okay when she's telling us about frogs and things, but today we got onto human reproduction and she went all funny.

MUM   You'd think she'd be used to that by now.

TERRI   Well, she didn't tell us it properly.

MUM   Well, you go and do your homework and have a good look at the book, then.

TERRI Oh Mum, we all read that chapter first time we got the book, it don't say nothing really, just people cut in half.

MUM Oh dear . . . perhaps you should show it to me then.

TERRI Oh Mum, you know all that. Did you know about sex when you first started?

MUM Started, what ever do you mean, Terri?

TERRI Going out with Dad.

MUM Oh Terri, what do you want to know that for?

TERRI Well, I want to know what it's like. It's natural.

MUM You'll know soon enough my girl. Here, what have you been up to?

TERRI Nothing. I ask a simple question and you start jumping to conclusions. I just want to know, that's all. No one will tell you, they all make jokes about it and draw silly drawings, but nobody'll tell you straight.

MUM I thought you weren't interested in things like that.

TERRI I want to know.

MUM Which bit do you want to know?

TERRI I want to know what it feels like.

MUM If two people love each other, it's very nice, it just comes naturally. Terri, I don't know how to tell you. I thought you learned all that at school.

TERRI They don't tell you what really happens.

MUM Look, Terri, it's just part of being married, you get used to it.

TERRI Oh Mum, people do it without being married, if they want to.

MUM The less said about people like that the better.

TERRI Didn't you do it before you was married?

MUM That's enough of that now, Terri. (*She takes a breath, starts again on calmer note*) You got anything else you want ironing?

TERRI No.

MUM What about that blouse? I thought you wanted to look smart for something tomorrow?

TERRI It don't matter, it's just Careers Officer.

MUM Oh, are they going to test you, to see what you can be?

TERRI I know what I want to be, Mum. I want to go to Medical School.

MUM You want to be a nurse, that's lovely.

TERRI No, Mum, not a nurse, a doctor.

MUM You don't want to be a doctor, Terri; you be a nurse, you can marry a doctor.

TERRI   I don't want to be a bloody slave, that's all a nurse is.

MUM   Language! And who was telling me five minutes ago she didn't get on with diagrams . . . fine doctor you'd make; it takes years to be a doctor, Terri, you'd be too old to marry.

TERRI   I don't want to get married, not if I end up like you, that's for sure.

MUM   You'll end up on the streets with your bags packed if you talk to me like that. Now go and do your homework and get your mind off sex.

TERRI   You haven't understood one word I was talking about, have you? (*She exits*)

MUM   (*alone, to the audience, worried*) I wonder what other Mums say. I know I don't understand all her ideas, but I do know some things, some of them I hope she never finds out. I even had dreams once too, but when I hear her say she wants to be a doctor, it's funny, it breaks my heart, but I want to shake her at the same time and say it ain't like that, look at me, can't you see it ain't like that. (MUM *exits, with ironing board*)

———

Scene Eight

Café. TERRI *enters, sets table and chairs. Three cups of coffee are already on the table. She sits. Enter* WENDY.

TERRI   Here you are, Wen. I got some for Diane too, she can't be long now, it's after six.

WENDY   You didn't put sugar in, did you?

TERRI   No, I remembered your spots. Stop worrying, she'll know what to do.

DIANE *comes in and sits.*

DIANE   Hello, Terri, hello Wendy. Been waiting long? I'm really fagged out. Mr Raymond made me stay on and do a perm for a client, some girl friend of his. I think he was still getting at me because you phoned at the busiest time. What's up? You sounded in a right state.

TERRI   It's not me. Go on, Wen, tell her.

WENDY   I'm late. Nearly four weeks late.

DIANE   Oh no! What you been up to?

TERRI   It was that party at Wen's cousin's . . .

WENDY   I've never been that late before.

DIANE   Why didn't you say so sooner?

WENDY   I got scared in case someone found out.

DIANE   Haven't you told no one else?

WENDY   I couldn't tell me Mum, could I? I'm sure she knows though. Last
night she came back with fish and chips; I nearly threw up. She said 'What's
the matter with you then — lost your appetite?'

TERRI   It could be something else, couldn't it, Diane?

DIANE   Might be, but you can't go on waiting for ever.

WENDY   What can I do?

DIANE   Don't get worked up, love, get a test. They'll do it at the clinic.

WENDY   What?

DIANE   A pregnancy test.

WENDY   I can't go to the clinic; me Mum goes there.

DIANE   There's loads up in town. The one I go to is called the Brook Centre.

TERRI   What, the advert with the feet?

DIANE   No silly, that's different. This place is specially for people under
twenty-five and they're not bothered whether you're married.

WENDY   How old do you have to be?

DIANE   Just say you're sixteen. They'll help you anyway.

WENDY   But where am I going to get money for tests and all that?

DIANE   You won't have to pay anything; it's free; just like an ordinary clinic.

WENDY   Ooh! I can't stand clinics. All them posh doctors in white coats telling
you what to do and sticking needles in you. What tests do they do anyway?
Won't it hurt?

DIANE   Stop imagining things. It don't hurt and there's no needles. All you do
is pee into a bottle, and they'll examine you.

WENDY   What do you mean?

DIANE   You know — inside. It's easy; but don't go leaving it any longer or it'll
be too late to get rid of it safely.

WENDY   Ooh, I couldn't get rid of it. I'd have to keep it.

TERRI   Don't be silly, how could you go to school if you were six months gone?
Remember Irene? She couldn't come back even though her Mum was
looking after it and she was really brainy, as opposed to you.

WENDY   I'd look after it myself. I can't stand school anyway.

TERRI   Huh, your Mum would be pleased having you and a nipper under her
feet all the time.

WENDY   Me Mum's never around anyway. I'd like to have something special at home. Just think . . . I'd be walkin' down the high street with a pram and I could knit lots of nice baby clothes . . .

TERRI   Oh Wen! You'd have to stay at home for years and years looking after a baby. You'd be like my Mum, you wouldn't have a chance to enjoy yourself again till you was thirty or forty, and then you'd be past it.

DIANE   I bet you wouldn't fancy washing all those dirty nappies and clearing up all the mess and being kept awake at night.

TERRI   Come on, Wen, you wouldn't have any money either and you wouldn't dare show your face down the club and you'd have to get any old job near home, not something you really wanted to do.

DIANE   Couldn't your fella help you out?

WENDY   I don't think I want him to.

DIANE   Does he know about this?

WENDY   Why should he?

TERRI   You're not even giving him a chance, are you? Maybe he'd want to help.

DIANE   Have you seen him?

WENDY   Yes, I've *seen* him.

DIANE   You better talk to him, love. You shouldn't let him off like that; it takes two, don't it?

WENDY   Oh . . . What am I going to do?

DIANE   You must get a test first. They're very kind and they won't tell anyone; they'll tell you what to do if you are going to have a kid and what to do so this won't happen again when you go mucking around next time.

WENDY   Oh, I don't think I'm going to do it again.

DIANE   Oh go on . . . Maybe you wish you hadn't done it now but it's not always like that. You wait and see, the more you do it the better it gets.

TERRI   Yeh? Who says you've gone off it anyway? I saw you making eyes at Mr Perry in Geography. Can't keep your mind off it can you? (*She giggles*)

DIANE   Here is the address.

TERRI   I'll come with you; we can go after school tomorrow.

WENDY   You will, won't you?

TERRI   'Course.

WENDY   Thanks for helping, Diane. I'd never have known what to do on me own. Don't tell anyone, will you?

DIANE   'Course I won't. Look after yourself, Okay? Ta ta.

WENDY *and* TERRI *exit.* DIANE *begins to clear the table.*

DIANE (*to the audience*)   I was like Wen when I was young; thought I knew it all. But I got pregnant, found out the hard way. At least she's got friends, and there are more places to go for help now. Funny, isn't it? A fellow'll do anything to get you into bed with him. He'll treat you nice while he's having a good time; but soon as you get into trouble, that's a different matter.

Exit DIANE *with tea things.*

―――――――

Scene Nine

Enter WENDY *who sits forlornly at the side of the stage while the singer sings.*

SINGER   Oh, the grass is not so green
And the sky is not so blue
And the winter trees are standing stark and bare
And like a bitter dart
There's a chill thought stabs my heart;
And my body speaks a warning: oh, beware.

Though I know the spring must come
and the barren branches bloom
And the stubbled fields with fresh life will have grown
It makes me so afraid
Of the choices I have made;
And the future I'm facing all alone.

For what will the summer bring?
Will the sunshine warm the air
Will the skies be blue and cloudless all the day
I've so many doubts and fears
What will happen through the years
Won't somebody help me find my way?

During the song TERRI *enters, comforts Wendy and leads her off.*

―――――――

Scene Ten

> *Clinic. The* DOCTOR *enters, sets chairs and table, and hangs up a poster of a pregnant man with the message 'Would you be more careful if it was you who got pregnant?'*

DOCTOR   Wendy Platt, please . . . Hello, come in, sit down. (TERRI *and* WENDY *enter*) Which one of you is Wendy?

WENDY   That's me.

DOCTOR   And what's your name?

TERRI   I'm Terri.

DOCTOR   I understand, Wendy, that you're here for a pregnancy test. It won't be ready for another five minutes, so if you'd just like to tell me a little bit about yourself. Can you remember the exact date of your last period? (*She fills in a form*)

WENDY   Ah — no, I can't.

DOCTOR   Well, how long are you overdue?

WENDY   About four weeks.

DOCTOR   And are you normally regular?

WENDY   Yes.

DOCTOR   When did you first start having periods?

WENDY   It was about — 'bout three years ago, wasn't it?

TERRI   Yes, same time as me.

DOCTOR   And you've never been late before.

WENDY   Not this late . . .

DOCTOR   Are you sure you could be pregnant?

WENDY   Well, yes, I mean I . . .

DOCTOR   You had intercourse.

WENDY   Yes.

DOCTOR   Did either you or your boyfriend use any form of protection?

WENDY   Well — I didn't.

DOCTOR   Did your boyfriend use a sheath?

WENDY   Well, I don't know, it was at a party, you see, and it was dark . . . I don't know.

DOCTOR   Does your boyfriend know you're here?

WENDY (*horrified*)   Oh, I haven't told him anything!

DOCTOR   Have you told your parents?

WENDY   Me Dad would kill me!

DOCTOR   What about your mother?

WENDY   Well, she's more understanding — but I wouldn't want them to know. You won't tell them, will you?

DOCTOR   Whether they are told or not is entirely your decision. All the information we get at the Centre is completely confidential. However, we often find that when parents do discover, they're not nearly as anxious as their daughters expected.

WENDY   Oh — I'm so nervous.

DOCTOR   Don't worry, Wendy, we'll do all we can to help you. I think the result of your test must have come in by now. I'll just go and see. (*Exit* DOCTOR *behind the screen*)

WENDY   Oh, God, Terri, how am I going to tell me Mum and Dad?

TERRI   I'll come with you.

WENDY   And everybody down the club.

TERRI   They won't have to know.

WENDY   'Course they will — you know what they said about Irene, don't you?

Enter DOCTOR.

DOCTOR   Well, Wendy; the result of your test is negative. That means as far as we can tell you're not pregnant.

WENDY *breaks into tears.* TERRI *comforts her. The* DOCTOR *smiles.*

TERRI   Come on, stupid. It's all over. Come on, you shouldn't be crying!

DOCTOR   All right then, Wendy, cheer up. Just let me examine you to make quite sure, all right? Now, if you'd just come this way. (WENDY *and* TERRI *exchange apprehensive glances. Then* WENDY *goes behind the screen with the* DOCTOR. TERRI *watches them go*)

DOCTOR   Just slip off your things and hop onto the couch. (*Pause.*) That's right. (*Pause.*) Now just relax. (*Pause.*) Very good.

TERRI   (*after a pause, to the audience*)   Don't seem fair. She's got all the worry — and he doesn't even know about it.

DOCTOR   (*from behind the screen*)   Everything's perfectly normal and you're definitely not pregnant. You can get dressed now. I think your period's probably so late because you've been so worried. I shouldn't be surprised if it came on in the next couple of days. But if it doesn't come on in the next two weeks, come and see me again. (*She comes out from behind the screen. To* TERRI)   Well, that's a relief, isn't it? I'm sure she's glad you came with her. Were you at the party too?

TERRI   Yeah, she told me when she'd just done it.

WENDY (*comes out from behind screen, straightening her skirt, etc.*)   Yes, but I never thought it could happen — you just don't think, do you? I never thought it would happen to *me*.

DOCTOR   Well, it could happen to any of us. Wouldn't you feel safer if you had some form of contraceptive?

WENDY   What do you mean?

DOCTOR   Well, there are various methods. For one thing, you could get your boyfriend to use a sheath. Withdrawal, by the way, is absolutely not safe. But perhaps it would be better if I gave *you* something, so that you wouldn't have to rely on him and yet could be quite sure that you were protected.

WENDY (*to* TERRI)   What do you think?

TERRI   Makes sense, don't it?

WENDY   What do I have to do?

DOCTOR   I think that for you the pill would be the best method, and having examined you I see no reason why you shouldn't take it. But you must be responsible and take one at the same time every day. And you must remember that you won't be protected until you're halfway through the first packet.

WENDY   It might get rid of my spots! But — what would my Dad say if he found out?

DOCTOR   What would your Dad say if you were going to have a baby?

WENDY   You're right, he'd throw me out. But — will it make me fat?

DOCTOR   If we find the right pill for you there should be no side effects.

WENDY   Oh — alright then.

DOCTOR   Alright, Wendy, I'll write you out a prescription (*She takes out a prescription pad and writes.*) Now: where are you going to keep them, and what time of day are you going to take them? I suggest first thing in the morning when your head is clear.

TERRI   Cor, you'd be lucky to find it clear any time of day.

WENDY   Oh, stop it, Terri. I know this is important.

DOCTOR   Good, I'm sure you'll be very responsible. (*She hands the prescription to* WENDY)

WENDY   Yes, I will.

DOCTOR (*to* TERRI)   What about you, Terri; you obviously understand how important it is to be careful. Do you need any help?

TERRI   Oh, I haven't got a boyfriend.

WENDY   That's what I thought — look what happened to me.

TERRI (*to* DOCTOR)   I — don't feel like it yet. But if I wanted to, I'd come along, I would.

DOCTOR   Well, you'd be very welcome, then. (*They rise to leave.*) Alright, Wendy, the nurse outside will give you the pills. Make an appointment for six weeks' time, and bring your boyfriend along next time if you'd like to. If you have any worries, just phone up.

WENDY   Thanks a lot. 'Bye.

TERRI (*as they leave*)   It wasn't so bad, was it?

WENDY   Here, I think I'll give Kevin a ring this Saturday. (*They exit, giggling*)

DOCTOR (*gathering papers, to the audience*)   I try to help them make choices so they don't let things just happen to them. After all, in the end a girl must make decisions about her own life.

MUM (*enters and faces the audience*)   I don't know how to tell you, Terri — I thought you learned all that in school.

TERRI (*enters and faces the audience*)   Nobody'll tell you straight.

DIANE (*enters and faces the audience*) The more you do it, the better it gets.

TEACHER (*enters and faces the audience*)   Well, what am I supposed to do. Sit there and tell them about sex? That's their mothers' job.

DOCTOR   I try to help them make choices . . .

TERRI   Don't seem fair. She's got all the worry — he doesn't even know about it.

WENDY (*enters and faces the audience*)   Me Dad would kill me.

MUM   He married me, didn't he?

WENDY   Oh, God, Terri, what am I gonna do if I am?

DIANE   Can't your fella help?

SINGER   We've been talking to you about choices
'Cause some day we think you'll find:
If you don't control your body
Somebody's gonna screw your mind.

THE END